Courage & Perseverance

Cordea Reid

Courage & Perseverance
Copyright © 2019 by Cordea Reid

Published by Cordea Reid
ISBN: 978-0578521879

All rights reserved. Printed in the United States of America

No part of this book may be reproduced or used in any manner without the express written permission of the publisher except for the use of brief quotations in a book review.

Cover Photos: Courtney Keay, Iver Gabourel, and R&E Media
Editor: Tamika Sims - tamika@inkpendiva.com
Interior Formatting: Effectual Concept LLC; www.effectualconcepts.com

Acknowledgments

This book is dedicated to my spouse Dwayne Reid, four children, (Stephan, Demari, Abigail and Gabrielle), and my cutie pie grandson Brycen.

I'm indebted to those who helped make this dream come through including my spouse who believed in me.

Thank you, Mom (Clover), Beverly Durant (Aunt Bev), and Marsha

My amazing husband, who has stood by me through it all, through the ups and downs and has continued to provide his love, support, and security for our family. Thank you.

My biggest thank you goes to my Heavenly Father and Savior, to God be the glory for all things he has done.

"For I know the thoughts that I think toward you, saith the Lord, thoughts of peace, and not of evil, to give you an expected end."
Jeremiah 29:11 KJV

Introduction

This book will give you insight on perseverance, dedication and strong-will. I hope that through my testimony, it can help shape your life, along with prayers and positive thoughts to help elevate you into your purpose.

It was not easy being a single mom, but having the right support system made the job easier.

So many times in life we go through situations that are not designed for our true destiny. Yet somehow we push ourselves into these trials and headache, all because we did not listen to the wisdom of those who have endured the pain and sorrow before us. Therefore, God has allowed us grace that we might learn from them to grow into the person, he intends us to become.

The race of life is a marathon, not a sprint. So run the race you are designed to run, don't let anyone or anything get in the way.

Growth must be intentional.

Stay focus and be blessed.

Love, Cordea

DISCLAIMER:

The events, characters and storylines in this book, have been documented to the best of my knowledge. Names have been changed to protect the privacy of some individuals. No royalties to be paid to anyone except author and publishing company.

No liabilities, nor responsibility is owed to anyone with loss of character from information published in this book.

Table of Contents

Ch 1: Going Back to Jamaica 1

Ch 2: Young Mom 9

Ch 3: Migrate to States 19

Ch 4: Sergio 33

Ch 5: Robbed/Graduation 53

Ch 6: Jamaica 63

Ch 7: Nasir 77

Ch 8: Connecticut 91

Ch 9: Pregnant & Alone 99

Ch 10: Dante 111

Ch 11: Stalker In The Building 123

About The Author 141

CHAPTER ONE
Going Back to Jamaica

"I can do all things through Christ which strengtheneth me."
Philippians 4:13 KJV

It was Saturday January 7th, 1995, when I landed in Kingston, Jamaica, after a nice long vacation in the U.S. with my mom. I traveled to the United States at least twice a year for summer and winter vacations. Somehow, this vacation felt different from prior years. I was becoming a young lady. I would be turning 15-years-old in a few months and it was time for my mother to have, the "Birds & Bees," conversation with me.

The night before my flight home; I was so excited to pack all my new clothes and shoes. I couldn't wait to show my sister's and friends all the cool stuff I got from foreign. Suddenly, I heard my mom calling my name "Finechild", but what made me jump was the sternness of her voice, it sounded as if I did something or something was wrong. I answered and went straight to her room. She said, "Sit down." My heart was pounding so fast you would have thought I just ran a marathon. She looked me in the eye, with all seriousness, and asked, "Do you have a boyfriend? Are you having sex?" I was confused as to why she was asking me these questions, but I was scared at the same time. I looked and saw the fear in her eyes. I answered, "No mommy, why?" She proceeded to talk to me about boyfriend and babies. I sat quietly and listened for what seemed like an eternity, once she finally finished, I realized it was only 30 minutes.

I went back to my room in total shock as no one has ever had that conversation with me. My mom left Jamaica to the U.S. when I was very young, therefore I was being raised by my aunties and uncles. I started thinking to myself. I have a boyfriend, but I'm still a virgin, why would I want to do that nasty stuff? He was my primary school boyfriend, you know the kind you hang out with at school, play games and sit with during lunch time. We were young and just having fun. That night I couldn't sleep, I was anxious and couldn't wait to get on the flight home.

I was enroute to Jamaica when I started to ponder on my mother's keywords, (sex, babies and boyfriend), telling myself I am not ready for that lifestyle. I am young and I just want to live my life, those issues are for grown-ups. These thoughts possess me for the duration of my flight. But, when I saw my aunt and sister at the airport, my thoughts changed to happiness. It was like a light switch was turned off in my brain. They were so excited to see me, as it had been three months since I last saw them. My sister hugged me and then grabbed the suitcases, I smiled at her and went in the taxi.

Since it was a Saturday evening, we decided to stop at my grandmother's stall and surprise her. When we got there, she had just left to get some more goods to sell. So we waited for a while. I looked over to my left and noticed this guy a few feet away staring at me as if he'd never seen a woman before. I was fair-skinned, slim and beautiful. Additionally, there is a different glow when you get back to the island. Your complexion seems cooler and lighter (LOL).

He nodded to me to come over, I shook my head in the no motion. He walked over to me and said the laimest thing ever, "Hey beautiful! You from here or the states?" I asked why, (twang), he said oh you a foreigner. I smiled and said yes. Suddenly, my grandmother showed up. She was so happy to see me. She gave me a hug and said, "Come pickney gal help me with the load," to me and my sister. He said, "Oh, you Miss Lynn granddaughter?" I said yes and he handed me a flyer and said, see you tonight.

While in the taxi to Denham Town, my sister said to my Auntie, "Finechild got a boyfriend." I said no in a childish way, but he's handsome. We both laughed. As soon as we got home, I started to unpack our stuff and show off my clothes. My sister was mad at me for one item, it was a red and black floral dress, (favorite color), she wanted it. We started to fuss with each other and soon we were fighting. My Auntie Shirley broke up the fight, and I ran out the house with the dress, my sister ran behind me outside, pretty soon she was on my tail, she pushed me in the back and I fell to the ground. I used my hands to brace myself, as I fell face down. To this day, I have a bruise under my chin.

She realized what just happened and helped me up from the ground, as I was bleeding. She was afraid of blood. We rushed to my grand-aunt. Auntie was mad at us, she didn't care who did what, and we were both wrong. She cleaned my bruise and told me to go drink some sugar and water. Back home there is a remedy for everything, this was one of them.

I was mad at my sister and couldn't wait for my mom to call, so I can tell her what happened. Mom didn't call and I was furious, my pretty little face was bruised, it's my first night back home and I was sad. Auntie came in the room and ask if I was okay. I said no I want my Mom. She said, "Hush Pickney, you be fine." Up to this time, I never had a bruise or cut on my body. Being a browning I took great care of my complexion, it felt like the end of the world for me.

It was then I heard my best friend, Tracey's voice. I regained my strength and get in a happy mood because it was party time. In the islands, Friday and Saturday is when we go to bed late and roam the streets. We would go buy chicken back with dumplings and plantains from Ms.

Lorna or fry fish and festival from Donovan in Tivoli Gardens on Bustamante Highway. These were the happiest times of my life, at least I thought.

My friends, sister and auntie decided to go to a party by the arcade. It was like 15 of us deep, ready to have some fun. As we walked to Downtown Kingston, we were having a blast, eating on the Street and just being young. Before we approached arcade, we had to pass by Matthew's Lane and Luke Lane, (scary area), of downtown. We all got silent and started to walk fast, as we passed a group of men hanging at the corner. Once we crossed over Matthew's Lane, we all let out a sigh of relief. Now we had to brave up a few more feet to pass Luke Lane. The thought crossed my mind, we were from Tivoli, opposite side of the fences, what if they recognize us and start to make trouble, what we going to do, we were just kids.

When we reached the corner of Luke Lane, I heard a voice say, "Browning, Browning!" I didn't look because I was scared. My friend Stacey, the loudest of the bunch said, "Who you talking to?" He said, "The foreigner." Oh shoot now I realize it was the guy from earlier. Stacey replied as we all keep walking and say, "No foreigner no deh yah."

It was then we could hear footsteps behind us. We all started walking faster, we almost take off like a plane that's how fast we were walking. He said, "Hold up, we not going to hurt you, just want to talk to the Browning." Stacey was like we got to walk back home, so we better stop. I said nobody is leaving anyone he's going to have to talk to all of us.

He said to me, "Browning where you heading?" I answer with an attitude, acting all big and bad, but deep inside I was scared. I said, "None of your business." he said, "Come on Browning you know where you are? You need protection." I answered from who? I can't believe I'm actually doing this, I felt like I wanted to pee on myself. He said, "You know what let me and my guys walk behind your gang?" I said, "Whatever," turned around, hissed my teeth and said let's go.

They followed us all the way to the party, watched us for a while and then disappeared. We were having fun, dancing and carrying on, when I noticed they were gone, not knowing what would have happened if they kept hanging around as they were a mixture of people from both the Laborite and PNP area. The party was over and it was time to go home. As we were getting ready to leave. I felt a tap on my shoulder from behind. I turned around and realized it was the same guy from earlier. My heart was beating really fast, if he was any closer, he might have heard it.

He said to me, *"You ready to go home?"* I said, *"That's none of your business."* He said, *"Cool Browning, just making sure you alright."* I turned around to my group and said, *"Let's go."* By now, I realize that I'm getting bolder 'cause this guy won't leave me alone. We headed to the taxi stand, no cab was available to fit all 15 of us. We wasn't splitting up, 'cause ain't no way somebody is going to hurt us all. We decided to walk back to Denham Town in the late hours of night.

Here comes the most frightening part, we had to go back from the direction we came. Stacey's big mouth, said, "Let's go," who is going to mess with us we from Tivoli Gardens. Therefore, we started walking back. I was a bit nervous, because it's now after midnight and we were walking through some lonely and not so bright streets. The place was quiet, we were quiet also, walking and watching our surroundings at the same time.

Just as we reach Luke Lane corner, we heard a noise, this area was dark, we all scream, then notice someone, walked out from behind a stall and he looked towards us. He said, *"Browning a you that."* I felt at peace and said, *"My name is Finechild."* He said, *"Yes Browning, it fits you."* He and his boys were waiting on us, to walk us home as close as they can. I looked over to my right shoulder and glimpse at Chennele and Stacey, they both gave me a smile, and that's when I turned around and said, *"Okay it's your life."*

We all walking ahead and them behind us, we felt more protected as we're still in PNP territory. The walk back was still quiet until we reach close to arcade. Then he said out loud,

"*Finechild, see you soon, get home safe.*" We all looked back and said, "*Thanks man.*" As we reached closer to arcade, several people were still hanging out, playing music and games. We were safe to be on this side.

We walked through Lizard Town where Sophia, Stacey and Sashana lived. We dropped them off and walked to bumps drop off Nickiesha, Sedan, Natalia, and Quanda. Next stop Bread Lane, for Michelle and Oneka. The rest of us lived on Albert Street right next to each other. It took us awhile to get home because we had to make sure everyone was home safe. By the time we reached home, my grand aunt, (Auntie), was still up, she never goes to bed without all of us girls inside. She said, "*Finechild, Betty, Chennele and Tamika you see the time a morning yu a come a yuh yard. Wait 'til tomorrow Clover call again.*"

Oh shoot, I had forgotten all about letting my Mom to know that I reached back to Jamaica safe.

The next afternoon, my mom called while she was on her break. We were outside since it was a Sunday evening, eating ice cream, at the top of our street sitting on the wall, talking and laughing with no cares in this world.

My auntie shouted out to us from across the street, "*Clover on the phone.*" We were a bit nervous because we came home late that morning and didn't go to church, (Yes, I been in church since I was younger), with Auntie, so we didn't know what she tells her so far.

Miss Chantal took the phone first since she's the oldest then we go in line and me last. As usual the conversation is the same question for all.

"You guys ok?"

"How school?"

"Everything alright?"

"Where the boys?" (I have two brothers Kenny and Mario).

"See you guys soon."

For me, it was a bit different (this time), because I just left the states.

Once it was my turn on the phone. I proceeded to tell her all of what happened since I got there in one day especially how Tamika pushed me down over a dress that belongs to me. As usual, mommy always tries to push peace between us. Mom, also was talking to us about being out late at night, partying and the boyfriend thing again. Oh my gosh, (I don't want to listen to this), even though we don't do anything too drastic, but just to be careful of our surrounding and protect our siblings. Our conversation ended as I love you guys be safe and love each other.

CHAPTER TWO

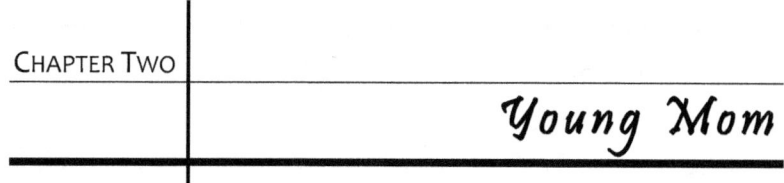

"In thee, O Lord, do I put my trust; let me never be ashamed: deliver me in the righteousness."
Psalm 31:1 KJV

It has been a few weeks since my encounter with that guy from Luke Lane. What crossed my mind at this moment is how things could have turned out badly for all of us. Sashana interrupted my thoughts, *"Where we going tonight?"* She came by to plan our weekend with the girls. We decided to go to Portmore to The Skating Rink.

We gathered the group a few hours later, and took a cab to Portmore. Tonight there was only six of us. The rest were on curfew for bad behavior the night before with other friends. We are all spoiled and well-educated, but also well-disciplined when we got in trouble. Most of our parents were in the states, so we were raised by family members. Our destination was about 45 minutes away from our home. Once on the highway we heard some very loud noises, it was a group of guys on motorcycle. These guys were bad news. We could tell by the entourage.

As we entered through the front entrance, I glimpsed and saw a guy just walking out of the bathroom. It was my stalker, (what a coincidence), I grabbed Sashana and whispered, *"He's here,"* She asked, "Who? *The guy from Luke Lane?"* I was a bit nervous at first, but then happy at the same time to see him. As my heart had been wondering where had he been. I walked over to him, (bold move), and his crew. His face brightened up as if the sun was shining brightly inside this dark place.

I asked him if we could talk, he excused himself from his boys and directed them to where he was going to sit.

I spent the whole time speaking to him, laughing and talking about our family and friends. Where we were from, it was just a wonderful night engaging with each other. Towards the end of the night, he asked me if I had a phone. I said, "No." He said, "I'll be right back." I walked over to my friends and was telling them what a wonderful guy he was and some of the conversation we were talking about. I skated with my friends for about 30 minutes afterwards, we decided to leave.

It was almost midnight. As I was leaving and heading towards the front door, I felt the tap on my shoulder. I turned around and it was Andrew. He gave me his full name that night, Andrew Thomas, AKA Nathaniel. Funny. Why would a guy give you his whole name if he wasn't interested in you? He handed me a bag. Inside it was a phone He said, *"Here's a phone. This way I can contact you anytime I want and you could call me too."* He smiled and said as he walked away saying, *"Good night my girl. My number is stored already."*

We started to grow in our friendship/relationship. It began to prosper in the right direction. We had several conversations about family, kids and what we wanted out of life when we grow up. He was three years older than I was, so I started to wonder how my family was going to feel about this relationship. I was attracted to his character and his physical body.

As time went on, we communicated more and more each day. I found myself being on the phone 'til the next morning, just chatting away. As a result of this, sometimes I would be late for school. Our conversations got deeper and deeper. At one point, the question of sex came up. I ignored it and changed the subject.

We decided to see each other one day after school. It was a Friday evening as I was leaving Gaynstead High School in New Kingston. I decided to stop by his stall. A stall is a higgler in Jamaica selling clothing from the U.S., England and Canada for a living. As I approached Luke Lane, I noticed that he was sitting in front of the stall and a young girl was standing in front of him. I felt jealous. I didn't know why because he was not my boyfriend. We were only friends. I held my head straight and walked past him. As I walked by the stall, I heard someone say, "Browning, Browning, Browning." I kept on walking. I never stopped, nor did he catch up to me because I was walking so fast. I had nothing to say to him, I didn't know who she was, or what they were talking about, but I was gone with the wind.

It had been three days since that incident. I wasn't answering his phone calls either. On Wednesday of the following week, as I exited out of my school entrance, I noticed a red motorcycle along the trees across the road. No one was there, but I had never seen it before.

I waited for my sister outside of the gate and all our friends so we could start walking home. Occasionally, we would walk from our school to Denham Town. It was about a 35-minute walk, but it would take us longer. We would use our bus fare to buy food, i.e., jerk chicken, jerk pork, or beef patty with coco bread. Today, we decided to walk a different route to get home this meant that we would not go to the downtown area to get home.

As we were walking, I had a feeling it was Andrew looking for me, but that little voice in my head said, you not that important to him, for him to come look for you, after all you're not his girlfriend. I snapped back to reality with the quickness as Tamika said she was stopping over her boyfriend, on our way home.

The very next day as I was leaving school, I noticed the same red motorcycle parked, but this time there was someone at the side of the bike with their back turned towards the school. My phone rang. I was struggling to get it out of my backpack. It was Andrew calling me. I hit decline on the phone pad and just as I looked up, he was standing right in front of me. I was like dude what are you doing stalking me and I started to walk away. He walks right behind me tugging on my backpack, "Browning, Browning; we need to talk, we need to talk."

I turned around and said, "I have nothing to say to you. You have a girlfriend and that's it for me. I'm too young to deal with this drama." He said, "I've been calling you for like three days now and you've been ignoring me we need to talk Finechild. We need to talk." I said, "Okay, so what's the excuse?" He said, "Not here," I said, "I'm waiting on my sister so I can't leave." I waited for Tamika to come to the entrance where we meet every day, so that we could walk home together with our friends. I pulled her away from the girls and said to her, "Tamika, Nathaniel is over there, he wants to talk to me. Can you guys wait for me?"

We decided to walk to KFC on the main and let him ride. While we're waiting for him, we ordered food and started eating. It took a little while for him to get there because of the traffic.

A few minutes later, he walked in and came over to our table. He asked my sister if he could talk to me privately. We both looked at each other with a serious face like *you know this dude is crazy*. I said okay, got up, and walked two seats in front of my sister, so she could have a view of us. Just as I sat down, he started telling me, *"I'm sorry Finechild you weren't supposed to see that and that's nothing you need to be concerned with."* So I listened. Apparently, he had a relationship with this young girl and had broken it off a few weeks before we met, but she was still trying to get back with him.

I told him I don't have time for games and I needed to focus on my life. Maybe he should try to resolve this issue with her before we proceeded with our relationship. I also did not want to get involved in something bigger than myself. He assured me that their relationship was over and he wanted to focus on ours. I listened once again and told him we would talk.

After about 30 to 45 minutes, I told him I had to leave. It was getting late and we needed to be home by a certain time once school was over. He offered to pay the cab fare for us to get home. I told him no, we would pay our own fare home. My mom, aunts and uncles always made sure we had money to do whatever it is that we wanted. As we were heading home in the taxi, I started telling Tamika what he said. She asked, *"How you know he's not lying?"* I told her I didn't know, but I would think about it. A few days passed since we last spoke. I called him and on the first ring. He answered. I told him that I wanted to speak to him after I left school.

We met up at the usual spot to have a private conversation about our relationship. We spoke for what seemed like an eternity. Set some ground rules about how we would communicate and what our relationship should look like. It felt great knowing that we both had the same idea of a relationship. I left that evening feeling as if a load was lifted off of my shoulder and all was going to be okay with us.

Since it was Valentine's Day. At lunch, most of the girls in my class was talking about what they were getting for Valentine's Day from their boyfriend. I left school that day feeling a little bit down, but as I exited the school's entrance, Andrew was across the street, with a bag in one hand and roses in the other. My heart smiled. I walked across the street kissed him on the forehead. My gift was a necklace with my name on it, with matching earrings, (along with red stones around the trim. Coupled with what seems like almost 50 red roses, it was beautiful. I felt so special at this moment.

Today he didn't ride his bike, so we walked to Devon House for some ice cream. We had so much fun together. We stayed there for awhile, then walked to Emancipation Park. We didn't stay there for long, we took some pictures as it was getting late. As we headed back to town, we shared a cab, he got dropped off first. We stayed on the phone the entire ride to Denham Town. I had to hide the jewelry in my backpack. I told the cab driver to stop at the bottom of Albert Street, so I could walk the rest of the way home. I had to devise a plan for the roses. No way my auntie or uncle was gonna see these. There will be more questions than ever.

Everyone of us has that one friend where their parents don't care much about their upbringing, what they do. So Sashanna came to mind. I went straight to her house on Victoria Street. She was in the yard washing her uniforms. I called her name, she looked up with a big smile on her face. I quickly told her what happened and she decided to keep the roses for me.

It was my 7th visit to his house when I realized, that I was getting more physically attracted to him to the point where I was ready to be intimate. We had the conversation again, he wasn't a virgin, (I was a bit disappointed), cause I had this vision of how I wanted my first time to be. He told me the decision was mine and he was willing to wait for me. I was shocked. I thought for a minute that he is different.

We continued talking on the phone, hanging out and seeing each other whenever I could get away from my families. The only person that knew about this relationship was my sisters, my cousin Betty and my young auntie Chennele. It was a secret amongst us, because we all had our boyfriend.

One Sunday as we were leaving our grandmother's house in Warika Hill, my phone rang. I ran outside to answer it before my grandmother heard it. We loved to visit Mama for Sunday dinner. It was our special bonding time with her and away from all the distraction when she trying to sell her goods. I told him I was at my grandma's house and wasn't able to talk. He said okay just stop by to see him sometime in the week when I can.

I stopped by his stall the next evening while visiting a friend of my mom's, to exchange some currency for me. Our mom always sent us US dollars whenever she knew anyone was coming down to Jamaica. It had been about a month since we had the discussion on sexual intercourse. He asked me if I wanted to go by the apartment so we could just chill. I never really liked to be out in the open and in front of his stall or friends, anyway. Don't get me wrong, they all had respect and love for the Browning. I said okay since it's not the first time that I've been to his place.

Today my thoughts were different, I was actually envisioning our relationship in a sexual manner. He leaned over and asked to kiss me. I paused for a second, smiled and said yes.

Monday March 20, 1995 is the day I lost my virginity to my first real boyfriend. The next day to my surprise, my sisters and friends were having a conversation about virginity and boyfriends. I kept silent because I wanted to hear what they were saying. I didn't tell anyone what happened the day before. I was shocked to learn that they had all lost their virginity. We met a second time a few days later and engaged sexually.

I left his home later than expected. Auntie was mad at me for being late. I lied and told her I was with a friend and the time slipped me. Before this day, I never lied to her. It felt wrong and I was punished for being late. I snuck away after dinner and called my boyfriend. I told him I was on punishment and not to call me, that I would call him and see him once it was over.

We continued with our relationship. Our conversation grew and we were really into each other. As time passed, my feelings for him grew stronger. A few months later, while doing physical education at school, I started feeling dizzy and nauseous. I went to the school nurse to get a check-up, she went on to ask me series of questions based on how I was feeling. The last and final question struck me the hardest. She asked are you pregnant? I lifted my head and answered no, I don't think so. She then proceeded to say that she would be doing a pregnancy test and would need to call my aunt to have a conversation with her since I was still a minor.

She called my aunt, but there was no answer. I was glad, but she proceeded to do the pregnancy test. I was nervous. I didn't tell her that I was having sex. She never asked so I kept quiet. I went to the bathroom and handed her the cup once I was finished.

I waited outside for what seemed like an eternity. The other students were in front of me. She called my name after about 15 minutes to come into the office and told me to sit down, she needed to ask me some questions. I answered yes ma'am.

- Are you having sex?
- Does your auntie know?
- Who is your boyfriend?
- Were you raped?
- Where did it happen?
- Was it a family member?

- How old is he?
- What is his name?

By this time, I was already crying because I already knew what she was about to tell me. I assured her I knew who my boyfriend was. I was not raped, nor was it a family member and finally, my Auntie did not know that I was sexually active. She told me that she would be coming by the house to talk to my Auntie later because I was at least three months pregnant.

I left her office, wiped my face, got my stuff and ran straight past my sister in the school yard. I ran all the way from New Kingston to Luke Lane to tell Andrew I was having his baby.

CHAPTER THREE
Migrate To The States

"God is our refuge and strength, a very present help in trouble."
Psalm 46:1 KJV

It was while running that the thought of my mom came to mind. She's going to kill me or tell me I'm going to have an abortion. In about 15 minutes, I was standing in front of the stall. I was very athletic. I did track and field. The ran was nothing to me. As I tried to catch my breath, Nathaniel was nowhere around. His friends were very concerned, asking me if I was ok. I said yes I just needed to talk to Nathaniel right now. I was shaking so hard I couldn't get the strength to get the phone from my backpack. Fredrick, his best friend who was dating my auntie at the time, called me over to his stall and told me to sit down.

He said, "Let me call him." He called him, no answer. A few minutes later, Nathaniel came riding down Luke Lane with a girl on the back of his motorcycle. I tried to get up, but I felt dizzy so I sat right back down. Fredrick realized I wasn't feeling well and he held my hand for me to get back up and helped me walked over to Nathaniel. I walked across the street to him and said out loud, "I'm pregnant."

To my surprise, he was more excited than I was. His friends were happy too. Fredrick said to me we got you Browning. At this time he looked at me and said you know what this mean? I said no. He then turned to the girl, "*Sis, this the young lady I was telling you about.*" I looked at her and said, "Hi." I pulled him away because I needed privacy to talk to him. He said to me, "*Babe can we talk later? My sister would like to take you to the house and take care of you.*" I was a little bit disappointed, but I looked at him and said, "Okay."

Just as I said okay to him, I fainted in his arms. When I woke up, I was in the hospital. Just then the nurse came in and told us that I was okay, but I was anemic. My body was under a lot of stress and it was too hot. Nathaniel asked if the baby was okay. The nurse answered yes and based on the information he gave her, I was due around December in time for Christmas.

As we left the hospital, he called Fredrick to call his girlfriend to meet him at his place. We took a cab and he told his sister Myrna to go fill the prescription the doctor gave her. I didn't realize she was still around because I was in my own world. Just as I went into the cab, I held her hands and say thanks.

By the time we got to his place, my sister and Auntie was there waiting for us. As I got out of the taxi, I looked on my sister Tamika's face and she looked worried. My Auntie was holding a bag with stuff that looked like clothing. I hugged them and walked inside the house.

Nathaniel stayed outside speaking to them, telling them what was going on. My auntie came in his room first and sat on the bed. She said to me what about Clover? I looked at her and said

I'm scared. I don't know what to do. Nathaniel came in and said what you are going to do is live with me now because ain't nobody going to make you leave unless you want to.

I told her I was gonna stay for awhile. She said ok, but everyone is going to be mad and scared of my mom. Tamika just stood there looking at me. Just as I nodded to her to come by me, his sister Myrna came in with my medication and some chicken foot soup. I drank the soup and went to sleep.

When I woke up Nathaniel was not in the room so I shouted his name, no answer twice. I got up and walked around a bit, I started to feel a bit scared now as I was never left alone in his house. There was a knock at the door, I jumped and asked, "Who was it?" On the other side, I heard a voice say, "It's me Myrna," so I answered, "It's open." Myrna came in with another girl. She introduced the girl to me as her sister Miesha. I said, "Wow! I never knew he had sisters." Miesha said, "We heard so much about you and couldn't wait to meet you." Apparently, Nathaniel was running his mouth about the Browning. My heart smiled. Now I had some questions of my own:

Where was his mom and dad? He never talked about his family members and I never asked.

How many other siblings did he have?

Before I could form my mouth to ask, Miesha said, "I know you got questions. We will be here all day," I smiled and said, "Ok." As we sat down, she started, "Our parents died a few years back on our mom's birthday June 15th. She and dad was visiting the country. On their way back to town, they had a car crash as they were leaving Runaway Bay. Mom died immediately. Dad died a few hours later. I sat still and listened as Miesha spoke so naturally about the incident. She continued on that they never reached in time to say goodbye to their Dad. The journey to the country was about three hours long. Nathaniel was in Panama at the time, buying clothing to sell. He came back home the next day, only to hear of the passing of his parents."

He was devastated and angry at the world and through this vicious cycle, he became overprotective of his siblings. Since he's the oldest, he would be responsible for their upbringing. He kept them safe. He provided all of their basic necessities. Bringing them to school. More importantly, no one knew they had a brother for reasons of his own. Tears were already welling up in my eyes of the devastating accident and how he was left alone with his siblings. It had to be hard for them with no parents, no other family members, except an uncle in England, who helped financially sometimes.

Unbeknownst to me, my Auntie Shirley already heard where I was. Suddenly I heard the bell ring as I was washing the dishes. I didn't expect anyone so I looked outside it was my Auntie. I quickly hid under the bed and kept still. Then I heard her say, *"Finechild, I know you in there, you better come out and not let me kick on this door."* She rang again, this time she banged on the door. I was scared. My heart was beating so fast because if she find me, any one of my Uncle's can and then they would beat the hell out of me. I have seen other family members get beaten this way, so I know what will come fi me.

After a few minutes, she left, then my phone rang. It was my younger auntie Chennele telling me that Shirley heard I was pregnant and she was mad and cursing. Auntie Shirley grilled them on who the father was and where I was. They had no choice, but to save themselves from the beating, so they had to tell.

I was mad and scared at the same time, just as the door opened. I hung up the phone real quick. It was Nathaniel, he brought me lunch, since I wasn't able to leave the building. He asked who was it on the phone? I answered what and why? I now sensed some jealousy. He smiled, handed me the food and said, "Nothing babe."

I got up from the bed and told him what had just happened with my Aunt's visit.

He said to me ok, I need you to stay at my uncle's place near Strawberry Hill with my sisters for awhile. I said no I gotta go to school. His reply, *"A few days missing ain't nothing."* He even volunteered to get my homework from my teachers. I was astonished at his remark.

On our way to the Uncle's house, I noticed it was near Reggae Legends Villa. I heard so much about this place, but never visited. This place is amazing, breathtaking views of both sides of Blue Mountains. Myrna asked if I could swim? I said no. She stated their uncle's house had a pool and jacuzzi. I said, *"Really? How come he never brings me here?"* Miesha said, *"You're family now, so forget the past."*

A few minutes later, the cab pulled up to a big house. I asked his sisters whose house this was. They both laughed and said it's our Uncle's, but we lived here. Nathaniel likes to stay in town, he only visits when uncle is here.

Just as we walked up to the gate, Myrna pulled out a key and announced a code in the key pad for the gate to open. I was having a real time movie experience, this house was huge. As we entered through the gate, we had to walk up a little hill to get to the house. I was tired by the time we reached the front door. Just then, the door opened. It was an older lady looking like she walked off of the pages of a magazine. I turned to them, "Geeze... how many more surprises you got?" They laughed at me to scorn and said, "Hi Auntie! This is...before they mentioned my name, she said, "Come on in." She said, "Hush! I talked to him already." She said to me, "Your room is around the corner on left." I had never had my own room. I had to share beds with my siblings, there was no privacy for any of us.

I looked at her and said, "Thank you," and walked in the direction she pointed.

As I walked down the hall to the room, I felt at peace, knowing they had accepted me and that my life had truly changed I was no longer a child and I needed to embrace this pregnancy and move forward. Just as I entered the room, I noticed to the right, a red couch with some baby clothing and other pieces what seemed to be clothing for me. I put my stuff down and walked back out the room.

I heard Myrna call me and said, *"We in the kitchen,"* I answered ok. I must have walked around the entire floor before I found the kitchen. They were laughing so hard that there Auntie said it ain't funny, so be nice. I laughed too and said, *"I never been in a house this big and this is new for me."*

Auntie Pat made some food for us, so the girls started to eat. She motioned me to join them at the table. I sat down and Miesha handed me a big white plate to eat. I checked out all the foods in front of me. There was jerk chicken, fish, festival, fried chicken, and rice and peas. Aunt Pat said, *"Eat up. Take anything you want."* I ate so much food that night I was sick afterwards.

Just as I was about to excuse myself and ask where's the bathroom, Nathaniel came in, they were shocked. He didn't say he was coming. *"Evening Auntie,"* and stretched forth his hand to take me to the bathroom. I told him I wasn't feeling well and I needed to vomit. A few minutes later, as I was laying down, his phone rang it was Fredrick, telling him that my Auntie Chennele wanted to speak with me. I spoke with her for awhile. She informed me that my mother was coming to Jamaica. I raised up from the bed in shock.

A few weeks passed and my family was still wondering where I was. I had moved on with no more worries. I had made up my mind that I was going to have my child, and the only person's opinion that mattered to me was my mother's. As I was walking around the garden of my new home, I noticed a car pulled up at the gate. Nathaniel came out from the back with a young lady on the other side. At first I didn't recognize it was my Auntie. I hugged her and cried. By this time, Nathaniel left us alone to talk. She told me my mother is coming down in a few days and everyone was panicking as they didn't tell my mother I ran away.

I was indeed trembling at the thought of my mother visiting, knowing that she was disappointed with my decision and would possibly beat me. I don't know where the strength came from, but I held my Aunt's hand and said everything will be ok, but I won't come home until my mother comes and get me. I was afraid to face my uncle and aunties. Additionally, I was a bit embarrassed because I had disgraced my family, by being the first one of all my siblings to get pregnant at a young age.

I went back to Luke Lane to live with Nathaniel, so that I could be more accessible to my family. I did miss them after all. Especially my Grand Aunt, I know she was worried about me, but I was too afraid to call her. As I was heading back up the lane from visiting Nathaniel at his stall, I saw Chennele and Shirley at the corner of Haywood Street and Luke Lane looking for me. I was no longer afraid to face them. So I walked up to them. Shirley grabbed my hand so hard, it hurt. I started to yell for her to let me go. My grandmother was nearby so she heard me and yelled, *"Let go Clover, Pickney!"* twice. Shirley said to me, *"You coming with me now."* She was so mad at me and was about to slap me in the back, when I heard a voice say, *"No Shirley, no."* It was Chennele yelling.

I turned around and ran back down Luke Lane to Nathaniel.

Nathaniel was very upset when I told him my aunt is going to beat me and she was heading down the lane right now. He held my hand and said nobody is gonna touch you, he didn't care who it is. We headed up the lane and as he approached the corner. He called her name. She turned around to face him and said, *"Who the bomba clot you calling bwoy?"* Nathaniel's response was listen no need for the disrespect, I just need to talk to you about my baby mother. I know Auntie Shirley wasn't the talking type. She likes to war with you and fight.

To my surprise, they were both having a mature conversation, I was shocked. I guess it was the approach. They started to talk like adults. He agreed to let me go back home as long as no one would put their hands on me. Additionally, if I felt uncomfortable with how they were dealing with me, he was just a taxi away. I felt so secure and loved by him. I never felt this way before.

My mom never came to Jamaica. I was only told this so I could come home. I found out later that my mother was sick and I would need to go to the states to help take care of her. Now I was concerned as she didn't know I was pregnant and I was starting to show a little bump in my stomach. How would I hide this from her?

My mind was racing. How do I even begin to tell him or answer his questions, as I informed him that I will be leaving Jamaica in a few days?

- What about his first child?
- How was he going to see him?
- When am I coming back?
- Our relationship, what would it be like long distance?

All these questions were in my head. I started to feel nauseous and dizzy. I called Myrna and told her what I was about to tell Nathaniel. She too was upset with me leaving, and not being able to see her first nephew. I explained the circumstances around the decision, and she calmed down, due to the nature of my mother being sick.

Now I had enough bravery to call Nathaniel to tell him the news. I called him twice. No answer. After about 20 minutes, he called back. I told him that I needed to see him ASAP! We needed to talk. I could tell he was nervous, I heard it in his voice.

We met up the following day at Emancipation Park, where we had lunch and chilled for awhile, just enjoying each other's company before I broke the news. My mind drifted away as I tried to envision our future relationship, and birth of our baby in a few months. Then I heard him say, *"Babes what's up? You said you wanted to chat with me."* My heart started to pound fast. I turned around and kissed him on his forehead and said quietly. I am going to America. He stepped back from me and said what his facial expression changed to shock, disappointment and anger all in one.

I stood still and quiet, waiting for his reaction. He looked on me and walked a few steps away. I gave him his space for a brief moment, until I heard sobbing. He was crying. I've never heard or saw a grown man sobbing. I walked up from behind and held him tightly. He turned around and all he said to me was, *"Why? Babes why?"* I too was emotional, as we held each other for support.

Just as I was about to say something, his phone rang. He ignores it and was very silent. It rang two more times, he answered as it displayed Myrna. I heard him tell her not now, he would call her back soon.

Nathaniel didn't have any words to say to me except for asking if I was ready to go home and if I could spend my last days in Jamaica with him and his family? I nodded yes afraid to say anything else, as I didn't understand why he was so calm. I had never seen him angry or upset.

Our relationship was becoming more awkward, Nathaniel was withdrawing from me. I would call him and it would be days before he would respond to me, and when he did the conversation was vague. I was starting to feel alone in this journey. My stomach was getting bigger and I needed new clothes. I sent him a text and his sister called back and told me to meet her somewhere.

Myrna told me he was upset with me for leaving and wanted his first child with him. I understood his pain, but this wasn't my decision and I was still a minor. I was devastated as the days past and was tempted to just run away again. I know he was acting this way to detach before I leave the island.

The last two days we spent together, it felt like old times. We spoke for hours about the future and our baby. Today was definitely like normal until he asked if I love him. Never had he asked me that question. I looked him in the eye and said, "You know I do. Of course I do. This is hard for me too." He pushed my hand away as I reached to touch his face.

He said, "Babe can you just run away with me and let's go to another country, somewhere? I don't want you to leave me. I'm sorry that I have to ask you this. I just need you by my side. It's just been crazy for me these last few days knowing that you're going to leave and I'll probably never see you again or my child."

We both started crying and holding each other tightly. He was really hurting that I was about to leave Jamaica so I asked him these questions, What would you have me do? Where would we go? How were we going to survive?

See I had a princess lifestyle living home, so I wanted my child to have that encounter to be well grounded. I wanted the child to be educated and well equipped with the information and knowledge that he/she needed to survive. Nathaniel had not thought about these things, so I felt like he wasn't truly ready for me to stay.

In a few hours, I was about to board a flight to the United States, so I wanted our last day together to be a memory of a lifetime. So I flipped the conversation, let's go have dinner together. He asked me, "Where I wanted to go?" I said, "Hellshire." He said, "OK, but we needed to take a cab, because he was not riding his bike with his pregnant woman." We both laughed at the sound of it.

We ate so much fish, plantain, ground provision and bammy. By the time to leave I looked like I was six months pregnant. Even Nathaniel had never saw me eat so much. I just know within myself it would be awhile before I go back home.

Today was a very unpleasant day. I woke up to Nathaniel the day before, lots of tension as I got ready to go to Kingston to finish packing. My flight was later on that day. I was hoping he was in a much better mood. Ever since we found out we were having a baby, we were no longer intimate. He was afraid to hurt the baby.

We had a few conversations on the topics of: How we gonna keep in contact? That I would call, write and keep him informed of everything with me and the baby. Baby names, if it's a boy or girl - the baby would be named after us.

When will I come back Jamaica?

It's okay to move on after a year.

This was the realist grown-up conversation we had since he found out I'm leaving Jamaica. We had grown into loving each other and expressing our emotions respectfully. I was getting emotional, this was too deep for my young soul. I excused myself and finished getting ready to leave his house. I needed to take a cab into Kingston. He called a cab. Minutes later, the cab arrived. He kissed me goodbye and told me that he loves me.

Those where his last words to me and it was engraved in my heart for a long-time.

CHAPTER FOUR

"Train up a child in the way he should go: and when he is old, he will not depart from it."
Proverbs 22:6 KJV

It was August 16,1995 when the flight departed from Kingston and I started to wonder am I making the right decision? Do I really want to leave my baby's father? It was too late to exit. I felt this notch in my chest and I wanted to vomit. Luckily, I had some mints to calm my stomach. Afterwards, I fell asleep. By the time I woke up we was preparing for landing at JFK in New York.

It had only been a few months since I last saw my mom. As I exited out of JFK airport in New York City, my mom and Auntie Amy greeted me with a smile and big hugs as usual. Nothing seemed out of the ordinary, but as we turned onto White Plains Road in the Bronx, my mom said to me, *"Are you going to say what's going on or should I ask?"*

I was becoming uneasy in the backseat, that's when Auntie Amy said to her, *"Clover, not now."* She just arrived. Her reply, *"We talked before she went down. Now look at the situation now,* eeh?" My gut feeling was ohh shoot she knows and they lied to me about her being sick, so I can come home. I was mad at my aunts, they deceived me and didn't give me a chance to make my own decisions. As we drove up East 225th Street, I noticed the area had become unfamiliar since my last visit. Just then my mom said we are going to a different place, I am staying with Papa's girlfriend. My mind was running wild. What happened to staying with my mom's friend? I believe it was near Manhattan. At this moment, I knew things would be different because my mom also informed me that she had three older girls, who is older than I.

What about Aunt Bev I wondered? Why can't we stay with her? I met Aunt Bev on my other visit to the States. She is my mom's best friend. She was a second mom to me. No other love had I found elsewhere, but Aunt Bev. She loves me unconditionally and I love her too.

As I exited the car, I looked at the address it read, 942 East 225 Street. A young girl opened the door to the building with a smile on her face. She motioned to me to come towards her. Her name was Carrie. I responded, *"My name is Finechild. Thanks for opening the door."* You could tell that she was very happy to see me and somehow heard a lot about me.

She pointed for me to go up the stairs and said the apartment is on the right. I headed up the stairs and behind me my mom was talking to her. She told her I am pregnant, so I need be careful going up the stairs. The stairs was a bit rocky and sturdy at the same time on the side. I took my time, went up the stairs and pushed the apartment door. Just as I opened it up there was a welcome banner that read, *"Welcome Finechild!"* Finechild is my nickname. Back home only family members and close friends knew this nickname. I turned around and looked at my mom and said, *"Thank you Mom,"* and hugged her as she entered the apartment.

Carrie ran from behind her and said, *"Let me show you your room."* No one else was home. So I thought it was only us, but the other girls were in their room, apparently not a fan of my presence. It was a four-bedroom apartment and me and my mom will be sharing room, which is ok because I have stayed with my mom several times sharing space. Even though this would be different, trying to hide anything from her.

I immediately overheard my mom talking to someone outside the room. I opened the door and realized she was talking to Ma, (my grandfather's girlfriend), she had bags in her hand. The names on the bags read Babies R' Us. She handed my mom the bags and went out of the house.

Carrie was very excited and somehow made me feel welcome. Moments later, the other girls came out of the room, greeted me with a hug and said welcome. We chatted for a while. There was cake, food, and juice. It was a fun night to be in a new home and to know that I'm welcome. I really kicked it off with Carrie and I thought she was going to be my new best friend.

The next day I woke up with a nauseous feeling. Just then my mom said as she entered the room, *"She's going to check on some stuff for me and would talk to me when she gets back."* She told me to stay in the room and call Carrie for anything that I needed. I was a bit upset although they seemed nice, I didn't know what today brings. And that was it, she left.

I got up and went to the bathroom, washed up and headed to kitchen. As I passed by the dining room, the older girl was sitting and eating cereal. I said, "Good morning," and as I reached the handle of the refrigerator, she said, "Your mom's stuff is in the blue bag in the bottom of fridge." This was awkward as I was never restricted to eat certain items, nor did my mom leave any instructions with me.

Just as I pulled back, Carrie made an entrance at the kitchen door and said, "Don't mind her. Eat whatever you want." I nodded my head, walked past Carrie and got right back in bed. I wondered when my mom would be back as I was hungry. A few moments later there was a knock at the door, it was Carrie with a big smile and breakfast. She handed me a plate with all the works; sausage, bacon, eggs, plantain and bread. She said for me to get up and eat. I told her I don't want any trouble for my mom and I know my mom will be back with something for me to eat. She said nonsense as long as I'm here you eat whatever you want, don't pay Shanda any mind.

I took the plate and ate it so fast. She said, "Dang girl that baby must be hungry." I smiled and said, "Yes we are." We both giggled at the same time. Just as I finished eating, my mom came in the room with an envelope and bags filled with groceries. As she emptied the contents of each bag in a small cupboard. I now felt that this is different from where she used to live. Carrie excuse herself from the room and said to my mom: later Ms. Clover.

As my mom continued to empty the bags, I asked her, what's going on. She said, "Finechild, let me do this and I will talk to you. A few moments later. Get dressed, let's go for a walk." I got dressed so fast and said let's go. As we left the apartment, Shanda came out of her room and said, *"Clover, you talk to Finechild already?"* I glanced at my mom and her reply was I will.

Something didn't feel right at all, as we exited the building it only had two floors so it wasn't long for us to be outside. We walked past a few houses in silence. My heart was throbbing. I didn't know what was going on. I no longer felt safe with my mom. Just as she started to talk. She said, *"Finechild it's going to be different here."* I listened as these words were being pierced in my brain.

- Stay in the room
- Don't touch any food in the fridge except the one in the blue bag at bottom of the fridge
- Drink or eat anything I want from the cupboard in the room only
- She won't be able to cook us meals, as before, but will make sure we have dinner on Sunday at a Jamaican restaurant
- She will be gone most days, but will get me a beeper or a cell phone, whichever is cheaper, so we can talk or text
- I must stay far from Shanda and Winiesha
- Carrie will take care of me when she is not around.

It felt like prison with a little glimpse of sunshine, but I can tell my mom is not happy here. It appears she has no other choice at the moment, this will be our home until better comes.

It had been days since I last spoke to Nathaniel, I felt like he was ignoring my calls. I would even called his sisters and friends. They told me that they hadn't seen him. He withdrew from everyone since I left. Fredrick went by the house and saw that his bike was there and he told him he's ok and didn't want to be bothered.

I was getting annoyed and frustrated as I didn't know what he was thinking, since I couldn't talk to him. My mom realized that I was getting in a bit of depression, so she took me outside for ice cream to ease my mind off the situation. While eating ice cream, my mom told me that she was not upset with me for being sexually active, but was a bit disappointed for me ruining my life at a young age. She would do everything in her control to make me happy and provide for us.

I would be going back to school on Monday. She would be enrolling me for school at Evander Childs High School and I would either walk or take the bus. She had too much expenses right now so I can't take a cab. I just nodded yes ma'am.

I asked her what's the deal with our apartment? She said the other girls is not to mess with cause they're mean and anti-social and not used to sharing the bathroom with strangers. I caught that because earlier, I was trying to take a shower and Winiesha didn't knock. She just entered and I was half naked. She slammed the door, hissed her teeth and mumbled as she exited, *"Mi a go late for work."* Both my mom and I laughed as I explained it.

She said don't worry about it, Shanda is the one to stay far from cause Shanda just had a miscarriage and wasn't ready to deal with it for months now. As a result, me being around will be hard for her and I must try my best to stay far. Ok, what about the not eating anything else other than the food she provides. It was a rule made since it was too many of us living under one roof, but if I need anything to ask Carrie.

Carrie is my new best friend and sister since my siblings were back home. I told her I liked Carrie. She reminds me of Sashanna back home. Carrie had mentioned taking me to Fordham Road to shop with her for a party. She said Carrie is very responsible and me and her will kick it off.

I told her I haven't spoke to Nathaniel since I left Jamaica. It has been a week since I last spoke with him. She told me she had a conversation with my auntie earlier in the week to tell him to call her, but he was avoiding everyone.

Time was against me. I was starting school the upcoming Monday. I was a bit scared and anxious at the same time. To start a new school with no friends or family and still no word from Nathaniel. I gave up calling or sending messages. My last message was that. I'm sorry I had to leave, but don't punish me for making the right choice, to have our baby born in America!" And I left it at that.

Just as I was about to watch TV in our little 8×10 room, there was a knock on the door. It was Ms. Catherine asking me if I was ok. I said, "Yes, I am." She then handed me a book bag filled with school supplies. She said have a great day at school on Monday and exited the room. I didn't have much interaction with her because she was almost never home. This was weird to me, my mom and I were just talking and she said she needed to take me to get some stuff for school.

My mom made sure I was comfortable within these walls at all times. I knew she was doing her best, but also worried about my transition to this new space and now I would be attending school. I heard the kids are vicious at Evander and it's very much populated with Jamaicans. I told her I can take care of myself.

That evening Carrie and I took the bus to Fordham Road from 225 Street and White Plains Road. I know that I needed to be aware of my surroundings and know the area because my mom would not be able to bring me to my appointments and schools.

As the bus reached White Plains Road and Gunhill Road, there were a lot of noises coming from outside at the bus stop. There were a bunch of children, (students), trying to get on the bus. They were shoving and pushing each other. Some were just talking loudly and cursing some Jamaican bad words. My thoughts were these kids had no home training. I am not used to this type of behavior, due to my upbringing, especially in public and around adults. It was a disgrace to hear some of the conversations.

Carrie looked at me and said, "Say hi to your new ghetto family at Evander Childs." I moved closer to her and said, if the kids act this way in school too, I wouldn't be able to focus. See my school back home was Gaynstead High, we were well mannered children, very respectable in our conduct in public: especially while wearing our uniforms.

She smiled and said you will get used to it. It seemed like an eternity on the bus, it took a long time to get to Fordham Road, the bus stopped at every corner to drop off these little brats. Yes that was my name for them.

My mom woke me up early that day telling me it was time to go to school. I was so tired. As I was awake the entire night reading

Sista Souljah's *Coldest Winter Ever*. I couldn't put the book down. Carrie bought it for me when we went shopping the other day. Besides mornings are not my best days, I would be puking for a few moments before I could get myself together.

My mom was never really home. I was basically living by myself, but she checked on me daily, hourly, but today she decided to stay home and walk with me to school. I can't remember ever having any one of my parents bringing me to school. As far as I know, my dad was never really around. He felt as if my mom is in the U.S., and she should take care of me. Back home I was being raised by my grand-aunt and other families. So this was new to me.

As we walked together in silence for almost half the way, my thoughts were carried away. I was thinking of Nathaniel as these thoughts and questions possessed my mind.

- It had been weeks now since I heard from him.
- My life is changing without him.
- Would it be for the better or worst?
- Has he given up on us so soon?
- Will I ever hear or see him again?
- What will my baby look like me or him?

Just as we reached Tilden and Bronxwood Avenue, my mom said that I have a Dr. Appointment later on that day and she would pick me up across the street from the school, at the Chinese restaurant and we can take the bus to Montefiore Hospital. My first day of school wasn't so bad. I went straight to the office got my schedule and follow each session closely. Most of the girls was impressed that I wanted to finish high school. I guess it was not common to or one just being embarrassed about their current circumstances. One girl asked if I was ashamed?

I looked around and answered, "I was not ashamed," to be a teenage mom, nor would I be a minority and not graduate high school. I was more determined not just for me, but for my child. And I excused myself from the conversation.

I felt more determined to continue my education, despite the stigma on minorities.

Just as I walked away out of the class, this girl Iesha said to me, *"You are really brave and she admired my boldness."* I just smiled and said I know who I am.

Iesha became my friend that day. She showed me around and introduced me to her friends. They seem like the coolest, yet materialistic Jamaicans. As I listened to the conversation at lunchtime, my conclusion is I wanted no part of some of their friendship. See at a young age, I chose my friends wisely. No one will get too close to me unless I let them.

The day went by fast, and I was eager to hear about my baby. As I exited those big doors, from the inside it felt like prison with a little freedom. These doors were scary to me.

I crossed the street just as mother said to and waited till she picked me up for my appointment.

We got to the Dr. office a few minutes later, due to traffic and all the stops since school was out. The lady behind the counter said to my mom, she will need to reschedule the appointment since I was late. My mom proceed to tell her it was her only day off and that I was pregnant and needed to see the Dr. ASAP. I think all the lady heard was pregnant, she said quickly, I will check her in and she would see me soon, to have a seat. I was a bit nervous since I hadn't had a real check-up since my first incident in Jamaica. Mom said I would have a sonogram. I asked her what that was? She was talking to me like I knew what was going to happen. I looked at her and said, *"Mom, slow down. I don't understand, a sono-what?"* She laughed so hard. She had tears rolling down her cheeks. I said mom that's not funny.

She gets ahold of herself and said, *"Today, we will know what kind of Pickney you a go have."* I was excited. I hoped for a girl, back home I had a doll almost my height, that I got for a Christmas present a few years back. She was still in great condition and well maintained. Looking back now this is why I wanted my child. Someone to love and hold, to talk back to me, especially moments when I feel alone and missing my Mom.

Just as mom was about to interrupt my thoughts of how I will tell Nathaniel, since I haven't spoken to him in almost a month. The Nurse called my name, "Cordea" I felt a sharp pain under my stomach, the baby just moved. I had never felt this type of movement before. It felt good and painful at the same time. Mom held my hand to helped me out of the chair and walked closely by my side.

A few moments later, a cold gel was placed on my stomach. The nurse said, *"Time to hear the heartbeats."* I lay still on the table waiting patiently to hear my little one. At the first sound I was in tears. My mom held my hand once more and whispered these words to me. *"I'm right here."* I felt a calm over me, before long as she continued to take pictures and measurements. She said, "It's a boy." Those words pierced my heart with gladness. I asked if he was ok? She said, "Oh, he's one healthy and big baby." I was in my 2nd trimester. I said what? This was all new to me. Mom said she will explain later.

I was happy and couldn't wait to share the news with Nathaniel.

Over the course of the next day, I must have called Nathaniel 10 or more times, still no answer. I was really hurting on the inside. Carrie noticed I had not gotten out of bed for school. So she came in the room and realize I was crying. It was only after 12pm. She asked me what's wrong? I told her I haven't spoke my baby father since I left Jamaica. She said what? What's his number? She also called still no answer. I told her to leave me alone and she insisted on staying with me. Just as she walked out of the room her phone rang, it was Nathaniel. She handed me the phone and walked out the room.

I held the phone for a moment wondering if I should have an attitude or just fake it. I chose to fake it. I said, "Hello." He said, "Who is this?" I said, "Really? It's only been a month and u don't know my voice?" He laughed and said, "He's playing with me."

I waited for him to talk. He apologized for not getting back to me and continued to tell me how he felt, he was really upset with me for leaving him, yet spoke so calmly. I swear I never heard this guy curse or get too mad. Nothing. In the midst of the conversation, I blurted out. It's a boy. He said, "What? My first boy." I hear him yell to his friends. "Yo, me a have a son?" He was so happy to hear about his child. We spoke for about two hours just listening and talking to each other. After a while, he told me he had to go and would call me later on or tomorrow.

I felt relieved to hear his voice and to know that he was okay. I wasn't mad at him anymore. I understood his pain and what he was going through. Suddenly my thoughts turned to joy. I started planning the baby name.

My favorite past time show came on as I turned on the TV. I loved watching *Family Matters* with the character Steve Urkel, (Jaleel White), he always makes me laugh especially when I'm feeling down. It's something about that nerdy and intelligent guy, especially when his character changed to Stefan. So I decided to name my son Sergio. In a bit of irony, who would have thought I would meet him in person on 232nd and Bronxwood where Estelle Winslow (Rosetta Lenoire), lived before passing on.

Life was going great. Me and Nathaniel was talking almost daily. It felt like old times. He said that he hasn't moved on as yet, still waiting for the Browning and I believed him. Today I told him the baby is due December 20 which was a few days before Christmas. This was my gift to him.

I told him I didn't know when I would be back, but I would asap. Once I get a job and finished school. I also told him all about my friend Iesha, he warned me to have the right company and not to hang out too much. Just as I was hanging up the phone, Carrie knocked on the door. It was a Friday night, that meant party time for the girls. I always stayed home. Carrie asked if I wanted to go with them, she will pay or me. I looked at her and laughed, "Girl, you see this belly I am almost eight months *pregnant and beside it's too cold outside."* She turned around and said, *"You coming with us, all you do is stay in that boring room."*

A few minutes later, she came back with clothes for me to wear. Carrie dressed like a tomboy so all she had was big pants and long shirt. These were the style back in 1995. Then she told me to put my hair in one. Carrie had some weave, she gelled and roller set it, then placed in microwave to heat. Looking back now I'm laughing, but this was my first time wearing anyone clothes or wearing weave. To my surprise, I looked great. I had a curly ponytail with baggy jeans and long brown and white shirt with some boots. I was a hot thang.

I had fun that night. I was very careful with the crowd and my stomach, but Carrie let everybody know I'm pregnant. So they were very cautious. We got home early Saturday morning just in time as Ma was waking up. She knows the girls party on the weekend, but never knew I went this time. Just as I opened the room door, she said, *"Finechild, Clover know you go party with that big belly?"* I turned around and said, *"No ma'am."*

She gave me that look and walked towards the bathroom. Now Carrie was laughing at me. We giggle for awhile, then my phone rang. Who could be calling me so early? I opened up my little flip phone it was Nathaniel. I answered with the quickness. He said, *"Hey whey you did deh me a call all night and no answer."* I can tell he was pissed. I fumbled to answer his questions. He asked again with a more stern voice. I slowly whispered a party. He went on to question me, *With who and if mi nuh breed. Party fi Pickney,* and he expected me to make better decisions. I just listened to him vent, till he said, *"Go get some sleep and call me later."* My heart was beating so fast. He was upset, but still spoke to me with love and respect.

It was a cold November day, just a few days before Thanksgiving 1995. As I walked home from school, I was feeling a bit tired, nauseous and really felt like something was going to happen. As I turned on 225th Street, I noticed my mom moving stuff out of the apartment into a U-haul truck. I quickly walked towards her and said, *"Mom, what's going on?"* She said, *"We have to move."* Ms. Catherine had moved out and we can't stay here because she didn't work enough money to pay the rent for the four bedroom.

I started to cry as I never experienced homelessness, especially in the United States, where I had no other family members, but my Godmother. To my knowledge we couldn't stay there, that's why we ended up at 225th in the first place.

My mother said, *"Gal hush! God will provide."* That was the first time my mother mentioned the name God to me. I was raised in a church back home, but I never experienced a situation where I had to depend on Him. Right there, I remembered my Auntie reading Hebrews 11 on faith to me as a young child. I said a small prayer, don't remember the words, but I know our situation was only temporary.

As I helped my mom to load the rest of our stuff in the little U-haul. We didn't have much, so it wasn't long for us to finish. She said it's going to storage, because she had no where to put them. We will go to a motel that night 'til she finds us a new apartment. I could see the worry in her eyes, with no one/where to turn.

Mom can easily go back to her living-in cleaning job in Dobbs Ferry, but where will I go with a baby? Tears is flowing from all the pain I thought I had released in the past, but my God is an awesome God. He said, *"I will never leave thee, nor forsake thee."* (Hebrews 13:5 KJV).

It was really cold outside. So we walked down to the Jamaican restaurant on 226 and Bronxwood. We spoke briefly about what happened. Mom said they moved out without telling her and the landlord called and told her. She can stay if she can cover the rent or she will need to move by the next day. I was hungry and didn't want to bother my mom, especially with all that she has to worried about now. So we sat in silence for awhile. I can tell she had no way out for us.

She held her head down and I knew she had a breakdown moment, see my mother has been through alot since living in the state. Some of which I was able to faced a lot of obstacles with her. Since I was the only child, that was traveling at the time. Due to these life circumstances our relationship is much more bonded than my siblings. As a result to this day, their is a lot of animosity amongst my siblings. I am Clover's favorite, because I got my Visa first. I'm lighter than the rest and the list goes on. Mom loves all her children and will do anything for us, not just me. All we have to do is ask.

I have never witnessed my mom at her lowest point. This was it. I reached across the table and tell her everything will be alright. Just then she held her head up, wiped the tears from her eyes and asked me are you hungry? I hesitated that was the least of our worries. We ordered some food, eat in silence. Not knowing our next move.

We stayed in the restaurant to keep warm, till it was almost closing. Still no plan of where we were gonna sleep except a motel.

We headed out of the restaurant and walked down to the park on 225 /226 Street and sat in the park for awhile. It was cold, so we sat closely to each other to draw as much heat as possible. The thought crossed my mind again. I'm homeless in America. How is this possible?

Just then my mom made a call to a friend and asked if we can stay there for a while. The friend said, "No." My heart sank. What kind of friend is that? I asked my mother. She just nodded her head, trying to hold back the tears. She said, "I will call Amy." The call lasted about five minutes. Auntie Amy said, "Yessssss." Thank you Jesus.

I was happy. I hugged my mom and said see God provides. She gave me a little grin and said come on; pick up your stuff. (I had put some of my clothes and backpack on the ground).

As we headed down to White Plains Road to take a cab. It was almost 12:00am and people was still on the street. NYC is full of vibes no matter the time of day or night. As we entered the cab, my mom told him 2661 Marion Avenue by Fordham Road. This was our new home. Not sure for how long, but for tonight, I will embrace the change.

While in the cab, mom advised me that Auntie Amy had two boys and only a two- bedroom apartment. She will give us one of the boys bunk bed, since it can't hold the two of us, she will sleep on the floor with a blanket, so I can have the bed. I looked at her and said for how long? She said she will get us our own place soon to just have patience with her.

I felt a knot in my stomach. The baby was acting up. I guess he felt the stress too. I was feeling overwhelmed and tired. I Just wanted to rest and calm my nerves. A few minutes later, we arrived at a building. My mom unloaded the stuff out of the back of cab. We walked up to the building rang the bell for 2b, the door buzzed and we walked in. Auntie Amy was waiting for us at the door. She said the boys are sleeping, but don't worry she would put the stuff in for us until the morning and we could sleep in the living room. It doesn't matter to me where we sleep, as long as we not on the streets. I was grateful that she opened her house to us.

A few days later and it was Thanksgiving Day. But just a usual day for me. Mom and Auntie Amy make sure we had a big meal. They had jerk chicken, oxtails, curry goat, fish, rice and peas, white rice, vegetables and carrot juice for the five of us. It was so much food, u could have fed a village. We had leftovers for days. We played loodie and card games all night. It was fun and peaceful to spend the holidays with people who cared about you. Mom was happy again.

Tuesday December 19- 20 /1995

On this day, NYC experienced its biggest snow storm since 1960. It was predicted to be 10-12 ft of snow. Instead we had 7 feet, 7 inches. The mayor called a state of emergency. As I walked home from the grocery store with some snacks and was feeling blessed that we had a roof over our head in the cold weather. I had empathy for the homeless especially in the winter time.

Whenever I see some and I have cash I will share what change I could as I looked back it could have been me. If it wasn't for the grace of God.

It had been a few weeks and we're still living with Auntie Amy. It wasn't perfect, but we were safe and out of the cold. We was blessed to have someone to help us out in our time of need. As I walked home that day I felt a kick in my stomach, nothing like I felt before. The pain was getting more unbearable. I called my mom, no answer. As I entered the building, I felt another big kick. Something wasn't right. I called Nathaniel, it had been awhile since we last spoke. He answered and I said it's time and I can't get my mom and no one was home. He said, "Baby calm down. Call her again."

I was feeling scared. I called again no answer. Just as I hung up the phone Auntie Amy came in. I told her I'm not feeling well, and I think the baby was coming. She said hold on and call 911.

The ambulance was going to take a long time since there was a lot of snow on the ground. By the time the ambulance reached me, my mom was home. It must had been close to 30 minutes of waiting. During the wait, mom was monitoring my breathing and contractions. I was in so much pain, I started to cry. Due to the snow storm they had no choice, but to make me walked out to the ambulance. It felt like an eternity to reach there because the contractions were getting closer.

The siren was on, and in the ambulance was me and my mom, she never left my side, always there. Again it took us a long time to reach Montefiore Hospital which was less than 10 minutes from the house, but due to the storm, they had to drive a bit slower.

I was in labor for over 18 hours, with no epidural at all. My mom wanted me to have a natural birth, the pain was unbearable, there were times I felt like I was gonna die either from the pain or pushing so hard. But that final push was my last. I screamed so loud that the nurses jumped. All while my mom was still by my side holding my hands and wiping my face. I can tell she felt my pain. As she whispered to me it's over baby, it's over.

On December 20 ,1995 3:05 pm, a star was born.

Name: Sergio Thomas

Weight: 8lb 2oz

Inches: 21

Mom: Cordea Holmes

Dad: Nathaniel Thomas

He was a big healthy and long baby boy. I was so tired as the Dr. rested him on my chest, I fell asleep. I was tired from that long journey to bring this miracle baby in the world at age 15. I needed rest, I was at peace with myself and my body.

Thank you Jesus.

Chapter Five
Robbed/Graduation

"The Lord is my shepherd; I shall not want. He maketh me to lie down in green pastures: he leadeth me beside the still waters."
Psalm 23:1-2 KJV

It has been days since I was discharged from the hospital. Mom had requested some time off to stay home with me. She was taking care of her first grandchild with feeding and changing diapers. I was still in pain. During labor I endured some perineal tears and had to get several sutures. It was painful to sit up, walk or even use the bathroom.

This was Sergio's first Christmas and he was only five days old. It was peaceful and quiet. Auntie Amy and the boys had left for Jamaica. Only mom and I were home. She cooked dinner for us and spent most of the day with the baby.

I stayed in bed for days eating, breastfeeding Sergio and go straight back to sleep. Mom was great to nurture both of us. I was glad that she was apart of this journey with me. The bond between us grew so much more.

Sergio's first checkup appointment was a week after his birth. I was in no shape to walk, much less carry him. So mom decided to take him for his appointment and give me the update later.

Just as she exited the door, Nathaniel called, checking in on us. It seemed as if that's all he did. I started to ask myself where this relationship was going. I wasn't working, therefore all of my baby stuff was purchased by mom and Aunt Bev. Not me and certainly not Nathaniel. I been in America for over five months and no money, just calls sporadically.

I was getting annoyed, just thinking of how he's going to support us. I never asked for anything the whole time since I left Jamaica, nor did he offer. So today I decided to make my demands.

Nathaniel's logic was absurd, he thinks because I'm in America he doesn't need to support us. He believes that life was easier here than in Jamaica. Although I had to inform him of some of the challenges we faced, such as not having our own place and that Sergio was going to need food and clothing. His answer was it's easier to send money to Jamaica than him send money to me and he was probably right, but as for me, I was done with the relationship. I looked on the phone and just hang it up. I had no time for foolishness.

I realized I was being more mature. I guess having a child will do that to you. Your mindset changes cause now, you have someone that depends on your love and nurturing to survive. Many nights, I cried myself to sleep. I was hurt and felt lonely and depressed. No friends, no siblings, just mom, Aunt Bev and

Auntie Amy. These three ladies were only my companion. Today I believe if it had it not been for these angels where would I be?

The conversations were not the same, in their eyes I was still a child having a baby. Mom was home mainly on the weekends. I remembered this one specific Friday, she decided to go with me to my appointment. As I explained to the Dr. how I felt. The Dr. said it was possible I was having postpartum depression. I felt no sense or drive to move forward. I just wanted to be by myself with my child.

Mom was thinking it was her fault, I was feeling this way. I assured her that I just needed some space and I wanted to go back to Jamaica. Maybe I will have a better relationship with Nathaniel. Plus, I will be surrounded with families and friends.

She ignored my request, but did advise that it wasn't easy to leave the U.S. with Sergio. I will need a passport, money, stroller and all these gadgets before they let me leave with him. He might be my son, but he's the property of the United States government. Geez I guess I didn't count the cost.

Today, I felt weird in my head as I was thinking about our future. How will I survive motherhood and graduating high school. As I walked to school on this cold January day in 1996. I was unaware of my surroundings, I didn't realize a few girls were checking my gears out as Iesha had pointed out to me.

I was wearing my new shearling coat, fresh new Timberlands and of course my mom's necklace. As I entered the entrance of Evander, this roughneck girl said to me, *"Nice coat."* I replied, *"Thanks. Christmas gift."* She smiled. Not knowing her intentions. I went straight to my homeroom class.

Later on after school, I felt the urge to walk a different route. As I turned on 215 off Bronxwood a few girls came out of an abandoned yard, I started walking faster as I recognized one of the girls from earlier.

Just as I lifted my right leg to walk even faster, someone grabbed me from behind. I spun around so fast to react then I noticed the girl had a box cutter in her hand. She demanded my shoes and my jacket. It was freezing outside, but I had no choice it was either to give up the clothing or to get slashed in my face. I only recognized the girl from earlier who said to me nice gears.

I willingly gave up my Timberlands, my shearling jacket along with my chain and earrings. All I was thinking about was my son. I had no time to think about these clothes and they can easily be replaced. The girl that I recognized from school earlier said, "To me don't worry you can replace it, it seems like you got money anyway."

I held my head down as I took the chain off my neck and just worried about what my mom would say, and just as I gave them everything they asked for, they ran off and I was left standing there for a few seconds.

To my surprise, as I turned around, a group of girls were standing there watching everything. They didn't do anything to help me. I walked past them with my head down as the tears flowed from my eyes.

I walked from 215th to 225th Street, 10 blocks in the cold January month with no coat or shoes on. Never in my life had I walked barefoot, not even in Jamaica.

The next day as I got ready for school, I put on four sweaters to keep warm. I never told my mom I was robbed, she would have worried and stressed herself out to buy me another coat. I dropped Sergio off at Aunt Bev's and continued my journey to school.

As I walked, I had to clinch my backpack, and put my hands in my clothes to stay warm. Just as I reached 211 Street, I saw Iesha. She asked, *"Girl, where is your coat?"* I lied and said I forgot it. She asked do you wanna get one of mine? I said no. I will be okay. Although I was freezing, I didn't want to wear her clothes. We both walked the rest of the way to school in silence.

A few hours later, it was lunch time. As I sat at the table with Iesha and the other friends. Iesha nudged me and asked, *"Cordea isn't that your jacket Simone has on?"* I didn't look up because I was scared. Next thing I know, Iesha got up out of the seat and walked over to Simone. I don't know what she said to her, but then I heard a noise as I turned around. I noticed they were fighting.

Then the rest of Iesha's friends jumped in. It was chaos in the lunchroom, (security guards), all rushed to break up the fight. I honestly just stood there. Moments later, Iesha walked over to me with my coat in her hand. She handed it to me and said, *"Don't ever lie to me again. I will defend you if anyone of them touch you. Trust that."* I just said wow and thanks.

As we exited the lunch room, the girl Simone was eyeballing me. Iesha went over and said, *"Round two if you, or anyone, touch her again. You hear mi Thieving gal?"*

Simone just nodded her head in agreement.

A few days had passed since the fight. Me and Iesha never talked about it until the weekend. Iesha had just called my phone as my mom entered the room. She asked if I was ok and if I wanted to come to her house with Sergio as she also was hanging with her son.

I explained to her my mom was home and on the weekend we do stuff, laundry and grocery shopping. She said, "OK," just as I was about to hang up, she said, "Wait! U wanna go shopping later for a new Tims?" I said, "No, not this week." And hung up.

Just as I hung up, mom asked, "Why u need new shoes? I just bought you some." Then she started to tell me these boots ain't cheap. She spent over $100 for it and wouldn't buy me another pair just yet.

I listened to her arguing with herself for a few minutes, then I uttered aloud, "I was robbed," since she was in the kitchen. Next thing I know, she ran towards me and hugged me. Are you okay? Did they hurt you? I said, "No mom. I'm fine. They just took my coat, jewelry and shoes, but my friend Iesha got my jacket back for me."

Mom had a worried look on her face, as I imagined she was pondering to move me from Evander.

As months passed by, I continued my day to day routine to and from school. Me and Iesha grew much closer with our friendship. Some weekends we would hang out with our children in the park and go shopping on Fordham Road. Life was going great until my mom announced that I would be attending University Heights High School to continue my education.

I was furious, my life was just getting better. I developed new friends, respect from others in the school and more importantly my routine to and from school, and learning the bus system.

Me and Iesha made a commitment that day that we will always be friends and hang out every other weekend with the kiddos. We pinky swore our intentions and left it at that.

My mom had a friend who offered to take care of Sergio, closer to where I was attending school. Her reasoning was she saw greatness inside of me and would like to contribute to my life. God had blessed me with angels along my journey with this thing called life.

Although I wasn't happy with the transition into an alternative high school, my mom assured me it was for my safety and I would be able to focus and graduate. I had to get used to a new bus route and methods of dropping off Sergio and reaching school. It only took me a few weeks to get it down pat. Iesha and I kept our promises so far. We spoke everyday after school.

She advised me that Evander is getting worst. A lot more violence. School was getting locked down and that several times guns are brought into the school which caused shootings. I was glad I was nowhere near that type of environment anymore. I guess mom really knows best.

She just about had enough too and her dad was contemplating moving her. I told her all about university, the classroom settings, my new classmates and more importantly, your child can go to school with you.
She was excited for the change, but she would need to talk with her Dad to move her to my school.

In the span of a few years and months, I was on the honor roll with a 4.5 GPA and I was enroute for early graduation.

I felt a sense of pride and accomplishment, that the stigma of underage drop out didn't fit in my lifestyle. Although I had a child it didn't deter me from getting my education. I was on cloud nine for the rest of the school day.

I quickly called my mom and informed her of the news. I know my mom was proud of me. that I also didn't follow the crowd by getting in trouble at school or with the law and or have another child.

For the rest of the school year, I stayed late, did extra work so that I can graduate in June 2000. A few months later, I graduated high school and achieved my diploma. I walked that stage, holding my baby on my hips. I was a proud mom with big dreams for our future. The future looks bright.

It had been months since I spoke to Nathaniel. So today, I decided to call him. The phone must have rung two seconds and a girl answered.

I looked on the number to see if I dialed incorrectly. Nope it was correct.

Me: I asked to speak with Nathaniel.

Girl: Nathaniel is not here Finechild.

Me: Who is this and how you know my name?

Girl: This is Nathaniel baby mother and I know your name cause all Nathaniel talk about is his baby mother a foreign.

Me: Tell him to call me and hang up.

That was weird. And I started to think how the hell, he got another woman pregnant, and he's not taking care of Sergio? Sergio is five-years-old and he never send me not even $20 to buy Pampers or food.

I felt some kind of hatred and jealousy towards Nathaniel. Had he been in front of me, I know for sure with that rage bubbling inside of me, would have stabbed him or did something crazy. I was mad the whole day, plus I cried and cried myself right to sleep.

Few days passed and Nathaniel never returned my calls. So I attempted to call again. I called twice still no answer.

Then a few moments later, my phone rang, it was Nathaniel. I quickly answered it.

Just as I said hello.

Nathaniel: "Baby, mi no have no credit so mi couldn't call you."

Me: "Bullshit. If you wanted to, you could have bought credit. I know you have the money to do so and what about your baby and your new baby mother?"

Nathaniel:" What baby mother? Weh u get that from? Cool no man. Mi have a girl yes, but she nah breed. You a the first, mek me know mi piss can bun grass."

Me: "Whatever, live your life. We are done anyway. About your child, if I don't ask you don't say or mention anything. You don't think he needs food and clothes? And I'm not working. I just graduated high school. So I can look for a job to support us. Cause you a deadbeat puppa."

Nathaniel: "Finechild, don't diss me like that. If you did deh a yard, you would be taken care of. Never have to worry bout a 'ting, but your mother want you a foreign so she must take care of you or send you back to me. Babes, mi still love you. Fi real you gonna be my wife one day."

Me: "That day will never come, cause I don't need you to do shit for me now or in the future," and I hung up.

I was determined to move forward without Nathaniel. All I had was me and my son.

Chapter Six

Jamaica

"God is our refuge and strength, an ever present help in trouble."
Psalm 46:1 KJV

It was June 7, 2000, a few days before my birthday, when I received the call that my job application for KFC was approved for employment. I was so excited. Now, I could make my own money for me and Sergio and also help my mom out financially.

I called my mom, screaming in her ears. "Mom, I got the job as cashier at KFC!" She was happy, but shocked that I was looking for a job. I told her all my plans. To work, save and visit Jamaica. She was happy for me. She also mentioned that if I wanted, I can join a susu, (partner), with her friend from 241st Street. I told her I would think about it.

I said, "Love you," and hung up.

Next call was to Iesha. She was in school, so I sent her a message on her beeper to call me asap. I went about my day happy as ever, singing and dancing. I was on cloud nine and to know I would start in a few days once the background check had been complete.

Who would have thought a little job at a fast food restaurant could turn their life around?

Thank you Jesus.

It's a new day, and I was still enthusiastic about my first job. Since I already knew my schedule, it was time to plan out my entire month, around the bus schedule for drop off and pick up for Sergio.

Once again, I was blessed with angels, thanks to my mom's friends who volunteered to keep Sergio while I worked. Most of my mom's friends loved me and they said that I'm very respectful, well mannered and very educated. I got all these attributes from my Grand Aunt Iris who raised us with pride and dignity. Although, we lived in the ghetto area of Denham Town, the ghetto was not inside of us.

I was always prophesied over. I was told I would be a great mother, my future is bright, and to just be careful of those around me. Funny as I look back over my life especially the last couple months of 2018, I lost some friends that I thought were good for me, but I know that God had to delay some things until they are removed from my life.

I always wanted to make my mom proud, so I made a commitment to myself that I would not be a young mom and a failure, because I have a child, I cannot move forward and be productive with myself or provide for my child. Therefore, I was determined to make this job work and do what I can to move up in the company and/or find a better paying job to support me and my son.

Time to get this bus schedule and draft up this plan on paper.
A plan written down is better than in one's head. It's my first day on the job and as I entered the building there was one cashier in the front and another team member wearing a different color. I'm guessing that they were a part of management team.

I introduced myself and they told me to wait in the lobby for the manager. I said, "Thank you," and sat down. I waited for about five minutes then the manager came out. He introduced himself as the store manager and that he will be training me today along with the girls in the front. I said great, I'm eager to learn. He smiled as he opened the door to enter the frontline. He then introduced me to everyone that was working the shift at the time, the cashier, supervisor and the cook.

We went over pay, hours and processes, then I was left alone for a few hours to watch several videos on compliance. It was very boring to me as I have always been a hands-on person. Show me what to do and then get out my way. After watching all the videos I could handle in one day, it was time for the fun and nervous part. I was hired to be a cashier, so it was time to show off my friendly bubble side.

It had only been a few weeks since I started working and my employer and co-workers said that I have the capabilities of a leader; honesty, integrity, decision-making capability, delegation and empowerment to others. I told them I was just being myself.

A few hours into my shift, there was a meeting called in the basement. This was my first team meeting. Our management team advised us on the upcoming menu, achievements and compliance issues, but towards the end of meeting, I was called to the front of the room. I was shocked, so I looked around to see if there were any other *Cordea's* because no way they were talking about me. They all laughed at me, I even started to laugh as I made my way to the front.

Apparently, there had been two secret shoppers in the last few weeks and they gave a superb review of my customer service and social skills with both team members and customers. But to my surprise, they both watched me for over 30 minutes after the order was placed. Additionally, with their recommendations, I was promoted to shift supervisor. I had to pinch myself to see if it was real.

Once again, they laughed at me and said, "*Cordea you're crazy, but we love you, and we all voted for you.*" Wow! I was loved by my team in such a short while. I never let my promotion get to my head. I was the same and probably better with everyone and everything. I continued to hold my head down and just be me.

Occasionally, as a Supervisor, your work schedule would be changed to nights and weekends and or opening/closing store.

Not having a car caused a bit of strain especially on the night shifts leaving the store anywhere from twelve to one am. Even though this is New York, the city that never sleeps, I didn't feel safe walking so late. Therefore, I would opt for a cab home.

I worked very hard to maintain my work schedule, plus being a full-time mom. Working 40 plus hours weekly and living a somewhat normal life with a child was hard, but I never dropped the ball. Even on nights when I am tired and could hardly deal with Sergio. To me it was all worth it, now I can buy what he wants without asking my mom or Aunt Bev. It was my commitment and the sense of responsibility that kept me going. Over a period of time, I was able to save enough money to go back home with Sergio. It was August 4, 2000, when I landed in Jamaica. I had been away for five years.

My first stop was downtown Kingston, right at Luke Lane to see Nathaniel, even though it had been months since we spoke. After all, he was my son's father. When I got to the bottom of the lane with Sergio by my side, I felt the stares of everyone on me. It was complete silence. It was so silent, that you could hear a pin drop. I was fabulously dressed with style and grace.

So I stopped and spoke aloud, *"I'm looking for Nathaniel."* Then I hear a voice say, "Finechild, that you?" I said, *"Yes,"* and walked towards him. I noticed it was Fredrick his best friend. Fredrick gave me a hug. He hugged me so tight that I had to whisper to him let me go. He was ecstatic to see me. Then he looked down and saw Sergio. He said, *"A Nathaniel son this? Man him big."*

I said yes and asked where is Nathaniel. He said hold on, reached for his phone and called him. He said, *"Nathaniel, Finechild is here waiting on you, come now."* I can tell by the conversation Nathaniel didn't believe him, so he handed me the phone.

I said, *"Hello, this is Finechild, I'm here with your son and you need to come now or I'm leaving."* He was silent for a few seconds, I said, *"Hello,"* and he said, *"I'm walking down the lane now."*

A few minutes later, I noticed him walking down the lane, (he looked the same way, with a big ganja spliff in his hand), coming towards me. Just as I walked towards him away from Fredrick. I heard him ask aloud, *"Is that my baby mother from foreign with my son?"* So everybody on the lane could know who I was to him.

I smiled as I looked over at him and see that nothing has changed. At that moment, I secretly thanked my mom for bringing me to the states. He hugged me and was trying to lean forward to kiss me on my cheeks. I gently shrugged him off.

By this time, all eyes were on us, but I didn't care. I told him we needed to talk privately. He picked up Sergio and walked away. I walked behind him as he showed us off to his friends. I briefly gave him his one and only moment, then told him I needed to go. He wanted me to leave Sergio with him.

I told him you must be crazy, where he goes I go. Besides, I had just landed and my driver is at my grandmother's stall on Haywood Street waiting for me. So, if he wanted to see him, he needed to walk with us back up the lane.

As we were walking, he bragged on us to the people who were staring. He said all the nice stuff in the world about his baby and me. I couldn't believe my ears. This piece of crap, who had never even send a postcard for his son's birthday, parading like he's dad of the year.

I casually smiled until we got to the car. I told him I have no time for his parading and stop making a fool of himself because he really didn't want me to start talking. He said, *"Cool, no man Finechild. Mi still live up the lane, come with me so we can talk."* I told him no. I am not going to the house, we can talk right here, right now. Since we don't talk much except about Sergio's well-being."

He continues to start an argument with me and ask why his son can't stay with him? Why mi a act like he's a stranger? I had to pull out my other Gemini twin side. Nathaniel finally gave up because it was a lost cause to try convince me to leave Sergio with him.

As I strapped Sergio in the car, he motioned closer to me and said, *"That's why I love you. Your feistiness is still the same."* I said whatever to him, and said see you later. As I drove up Albert Street, every one was watching the vehicle because they had never seen that vehicle in the area before. After passing a few yards, (government houses), I told the driver to stop at 16 Albert Street. As I exited the car, I heard someone said Finechild. I looked around and saw that it was my cousin Betty. She helped me with my luggages, while I monitor Sergio.

I walked in the yard, the majority of my family were there. They all gave me a big hug and was so happy to see us. I was ecstatic too, it had been over five years since I last saw them. I settled in for a few minutes, unpacked my stuff, and removed all the clothing that I had bought for some of my families and few of my friends. My sisters and brothers were at school, so they were the last to know I was home. I was famished, so I asked my auntie if Miss Lorna was still selling fried chicken back and plantains. She said yes. I asked Betty to walked with me.

As I walked up Albert Street, everyone was stopping me to chat and see the baby. I was trying to be polite and reconnect. It had taken over one hour to go and get food. As I stepped in Miss

Lorna's yard, the crowd got quiet and a few of them turned towards me. I noticed everything was the same as usual. I waited for a little, then Sergio started crying from all the noise around him. So Miss Lorna asked me what I wanted, I ordered a lot of food, (to feed five or more people). I thanked everyone, paid and received my food.

I could not wait to reach Albert Street, so I told Betty to hold Sergio's hand. As I took a piece of chicken back out and started to eat, it was just like back in the days. Everyone on the road was looking at me as I tore the food apart, saying, "mmmm." I was in Heaven and didn't care. The food was so good. I ate that meat like I had not had a meal in years.

Just as I turned the corner on Albert Street, my sisters were coming toward me. The second oldest one Tameka, shoved me and say, "*Red Gal, (someone of lighter complexion), you come back a yuh yard?*" I smiled and hugged them both, but said out loud watch my food. There are two things about me that you should never mess with, my food and me. When I'm tired, I am grumpier than an old woman.

The four of us walked back down the street, just like old times. Again everyone was staring. I wasn't the skinny Finechild anymore, I was Fatchild, (I gained about 40 pounds), but it looked good on me. My sister and aunts were grilling me about Nathaniel. If him see Sergio yet? I told them I stopped by before coming to the house. He was just as surprised as they were. Plus, he wanted to keep him for awhile. I informed them I told him no. He can see him when I'm around.

They all got mad at me and say a crazy thing, I am doing. He deserve to see him pickney. I just let them have it about what I went through and how he was not there emotionally, mentally, not to mention, financially. As far as I was concerned, he was just a sperm donor.

They said Finechild you cold. My response, *"I don't care enough about Nathaniel."* I wanna have fun and since it was a Friday night, where we going? We all laughed. It was no more tensions. Time to party.

We had so much fun last night, we went by Donovan and got some fried fish and festival, then walked through Tivoli Gardens to go by Auntie Shirley house. Afterwards, we headed to a street dance in the area for a few hours. I was dancing and just being me, (free), just living a little. Having a baby at a young age, I missed out on some of the fun of growing. It wasn't long until I was noticed by one of the bad men in the area. He had sent one of his boys over to call me. I informed the young guy, I am not going anywhere.

Just as he walked away, I turned to my cousin and asked who was that? She said what he said to you? I told her he said, *"Preston call me."* She said, *"What?"* I repeat it and she said to me lets get out of here. Apparently, something was wrong, we signaled the others to leave. Just as I was near to bumps, (an area of Tivoli Garden) I felt a hand grab me from behind. I turned around only to notice this man on a bicycle with an entourage behind him.

I said, "Let me go."

Preston: "No from your young mi a watch you. Now you a big woman, me want you."

Me: "Hell no! I don't care who or what you are, you gonna have to shoot me tonight cause mi not leaving with you."

Preston: "Ok."

Me: I looked around real quick and grab unto a piece of the iron rail. I held it so tight on my first grab.

Preston: "Finechild, let go."

Me: "No, I'm not going with you to possibly rape and kill me. Leave mi alone."

Preston: "Mi done talk."

Then he tells everyone to leave us alone.

All my family and friends said they not leaving me, he's going have to kill all of us. He then slapped me in my face. I screamed out so loud, so that one of his guys said to him leave her alone, lets go. That's when one of my cousin's left us and ran back into Tivoli. I became very afraid, this man was not letting me go.

A few minutes later, my cousin came back on a bike, with a man. He rolled up beside Preston, whispered something in his ears, and in a few seconds, he let me go. Then Preston said to me there will be a next time. The man then asked me, "*Where you going?*" I told him Albert Street, then he motioned to me to come on the bike. I looked on my cousin and family, they said it's okay.

I then got on, while Preston was standing there. My family say they will meet me there. The ride was silent, until I got to the front of our yard. I got off, said thanks and walked away. He then called me back and said, *"Don't worry, he won't bother you again."* I told him I was scared. All my years living in Jamaica nothing like this ever happened so why now. He said it's cool, we will take care of it.

Last night was crazy, I was afraid for my life and as I lay awake in bed with my son beside me, I wondered what could have happened if the guy didn't come to save me. I was afraid to leave the house. I was ready to be on the next flight back to New York.

A few minutes later, my siblings and cousin came in the room. We are all silent, then one of them asked you ok. I said, *"Hell no! I'm ready to leave this place. How do I tell mommy and the family what happened last night? And who was that man?"*

My cousin then asked me, *"You don't know him?"* I said, *"No."* She said, *"Really Finechild?"* Suddenly, my sister said, *"That the Don fi the area."* I was in shock. I was that close to him. Wow this was really bad.

I got up quickly and started packing my stuff, then they all laughed at me saying watch the scared gal. I told them I don't care who or what they were saying, I'm leaving. Just then Auntie came in the room, apparently she heard something. She asked, *"You ok Finechild and what happened?"* I looked at the family, then said nothing. She then said to me, don't worry I know who to go talk to. Get up and go enjoy yourself, I will take care of it.

So, I just sat on the bed and started crying. I didn't want any problems for my family, especially since I don't live here anymore. My cousin and sisters consoled and commanded me to stop acting like an idiot. I needed to go take a bath. It's Saturday and besides Nathaniel want to see me.

I was so used to him not being around, that even being here I didn't feel the need to be around him.

Today I was in no mood to talk to and or see Nathaniel, but I had no choice since it's my second day being in Jamaica. I know that he needed to see Sergio and have a conversation with me. Therefore, I decided to just go and get it over with. I get Sergio something to eat and we decided to walk the area.

It had been a long time since I saw the culture of the markets. As I walked through Coronation Market, I noticed it was more crowded, smelly and dirty. As I got deeper and deeper into the market, my cousin told me to put my purse in front of me because they will try to rob me. I was like really? What happened to all the fun times we had walking through this area with no issues.

A few minutes later, we arrived where Nathaniel was selling his clothing. Just as I walked closer up the lane, I saw him with a pregnant girl beside him. As I got closer, I uttered aloud, *"Nathaniel see your son here."* The girl then looked at him and then looked at me and Sergio.

He introduced us to her, *"Chanelle this is Finechild and my son Sergio."* She then said to him, *"Yes, I know, I heard she was here,"* and then walked away. I just looked at her and hissed my teeth. I couldn't care less about her feelings. I'm here now, so it's Sergio's time we're only here for a short while, so girl bye, I have no time for drama.

Nathaniel looked at me and say, *"You see the respect she just give you? None of my other baby mothers can step to her like that, else a war."* I said, *"Wait! What other baby mothers? How many you have?"* He smiled and said, *"Three, but you the first, and everybody knows that. Nobody can touch you."*

I just stood there in disbelief. All the love I had for this man, and all the past pain and hurts just flashed through my mind. I was confused and mad at the same time. All these years, I was saving myself for him and he just went on with his life.

I then said to him, *"I honestly thought we could have talked things over, make amends and move forward, but my eyes are completely wide open. I see you for who and what you are and I don't want any part of it. You can have a relationship with your child if you choose to do so."* I then gave him my number, handed Sergio to him and walked towards my family. I was hurt, plus I was trying really hard to hold back my tears. As I walked away, he said, *"Don't blame me baby, blame your mom, she didn't want us to be together. I will always love you Finechild, but after, all I'm a man."* I then handed Sergio's backpack to my cousin and asked her to stay with him. I think that they all heard the tremble in my voice. They asked if I was ok. I told them I would be fine, I'm a strong woman and then walked away.

Over the next few days, I decided to just have fun and let loose because I didn't know when I'd be coming back to Jamaica again. Therefore, I planned what I wanted to do each and everyday, where I wanted to go, the food that I wanted to eat, not just for myself or with my sisters and cousin. By this time, I didn't have many friends left in the area, most of them graduated high school and went on to the States or moved to a different part of Jamaica.

We visited several places like Port Royal, Dunn's River Falls, Emancipation Park, Bob Marley Museum and Devon House. These places are apart of Jamaica's Heritage. I didn't bring Sergio outside much with me, he just wanted to stay in the house with Auntie and play with the children in the area, playing his favorite sport, football. The two weeks in Jamaica went by quick. I ate so much food and enjoyed my families and friends. I know I spent a fortune on my trip, but it was all worth it.

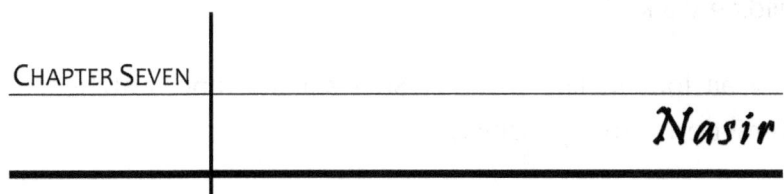

Chapter Seven

Nasir

> *"There is no fear in love; but perfect love casteth out fear: because fear hath torment. He that feareth is not made perfect in love."*
> 1 John 4:18 KJV

It was at this moment, I realized that my mom had moved closer to my job on 238 White Plains Road. Since I had an extra day, I helped her unpack and relax the rest of the day, before going back to reality.

As I exited my building, a group of guys were hanging outside in front of the steps. I had to say excuse me twice. On my second time saying this, I heard one of them say, *"Oh, I never see you in this building."* I held my head straight and walked pass them to work. My co-workers were excited to see me. I had brought back a few treats, (bun, banana chips and beef patty), from Jamaica for them. I shared it evenly amongst them prior to starting my shift.

I relieved my manager on duty in less than thirty minutes. We talked about new policies and procedures. Since it was a Monday afternoon and the store was slow, I decided to sit in the lobby. As I sat down, a few of the guys from in front of the building walked in.

They all looked like trouble. So I sat still and watched their interaction with my cashier.

It must have taken them nearly 20 minutes to decide and order their meals. I counted seven of them, so I decided to help packed meals. I got up and just as I reached the door handle one of them said, *"See her there, she mi want pack my food."*

I pretended not to hear him, so I entered the office, washed my hands, put on gloves and started packing. It took both of us under three minutes to pack all orders. Yes, I didn't just delegate, I helped my team. Just as I repeated the last order, I noticed this guy was finer than the rest. He seemed much calmer and humble. He smiled at me and said, *"Thanks."*

Just as they exited the door, I looked at my cashier as she glanced back at me and said, *"All they want is free food."* Then we both laughed, and went onto the next customer. I'm used to guys flirting with me especially on the job for free food or they were looking for a woman to take care of them. My mind was focused on me and my son, so a boyfriend was the last thing in my head, but there was something about that last guy that sparked my interest.

A few days later as I exited the building to head to work, I noticed that it was the same set of guys sitting outside smoking weed and just hanging out. The weather was still warm, so a lot of people were hanging outside the building.

I wasn't used to this because, when I was living on Marion Avenue and Bronxwood, people were not hanging outside the building 'til late at night. It was my night to close, so I was secretly hoping they'll not be here when I leave work after 12 am in the morning. I hated the closing of the store, not because it requires more work, but the inconsistencies of the time you will leave at night or early next day.

As I passed them, I felt a tap on my shoulder. I looked around and said to him you brave. You don't know me, so don't touch me. His reply, "*I know you enough to know that you are a strong woman who takes care of your son.*" I let my guard down just a tiny bit. I said, "*Oh yes, I have to do it 'cause no one else will.*"

He asked if he could walk with me to work, I said sure. We conversed for the short walk which was only three blocks, and in such a small time, he told me he's been watching me since he saw me the first day, (when I got out of the cab back from Jamaica).

He told me about his girls in Jamaica and how they are his pride and joy. And he hoped to see them soon. He asked for my number, I hesitated a bit, then said sure why not. It wouldn't hurt to have a friend. We exchanged numbers and promised to call each other later. However, I didn't make the first call that night as I was nervous and shy. It had been a long time since I let anyone in. I was still heartbroken over Nathaniel.

Again, as I exited the building to go to work, the same set of guys were still standing outside. It seems as if that's all they did was hang outside. I was secretly looking for Nasir, but he wasn't there. I was hoping to see him there so I wouldn't have to call him.

I was a little bit disappointed, so I just held my head high, and walked past the guys and went on my merry way to work. As I entered the restaurant door, I looked through the glass and realized Nasir was sitting down waiting for me. I was shocked. Why is he here I wondered? I always try to reach work at least 15 minutes early, so I have time to connect with my team and once I begin working, no chit chatting. But today a new convo awaited me.

I opened the door with a little smirk on my face. I walked up to him and sat in the back of the restaurant. He asked me if everything is okay? I said, *"Yes, you just wanted to see me since I didn't call you last night."* I told him that I was busy and by the time I left work, it was too late to call him. He smiled and said, *"You could call me anytime you want to talk."*

I told him I don't have much time because I needed to get on the clock. He then asked me what time I'm leaving work? I told him I'm not sure, but I know I'm closing so it's going to be late. He then said to me he'll be here before the store closed, so he could walk me home.

I said thank you, then got up and said see you later and went in to start work.

My co-workers that were on staff were all looking at me. One of them said, "He had been there for awhile, we didn't know he was waiting for you. I was like really he waited a long time?" Then my manager said to me, *"Cordea got a boyfriend."*

I said, *"No, he's just a friend for now."*

Over the next few weeks, we became close friends. There were several times that while I'm at work, he would come by to visit and wait to walk me home late at night. This night was different, I noticed he was not his usual playful self. He told me that his sister had just moved out of the apartment and he would be moving closer up this side with a few friends for awhile. I was happy at the thought of him moving closer because taking the train to Allerton was a few stops away from me.

I didn't want to get involved in the family part, so I just asked if he needed my help to move. He said not really, but it would be nice to have me around. I told him I would be off in a few days and then I can help. We continued walking in silence, until his phone rang. It was one of his daughter's in Jamaica calling. So I leaned over and whispered in his ears, *I will be fine. Go take care of family.* Then I let his hands go and continued walking home.

Somehow I felt his loneliness and pain, but there was not much that I could do at this moment. I waited for a few hours then sent him a text to let him know everything will be alright.

I kept my promise that to help him that weekend. When I get to the apartment by Allerton, I realized that he didn't have much. He didn't even have a bed. All he had was his clothes. I could tell that he was a little bit embarrassed when I saw that he did not have a bed. Then he said to me that his sister took everything, therefore so he would have to start all over. My first thought is what kind of sister would leave her brother like that? But there are always two sides to a story.

I kept quiet and helped clean up the apartment. We carried the few items he had downstairs into the cab. We then proceeded to his cousin's house on Pitman Avenue. When we got to the cousin's house, I noticed he was leaving his stuff in the basement. I asked him where was his room? He didn't answer, so I just said to him where to after we leave here.

Then I noticed a shift in his voice, he said, *"I will walk you home."* I was shocked by his persona. He was a bit different with his tone and attitude. So, I said ok and walked past him and sat outside. A few minutes later, two guys came down to the basement door and asked for him. I said he's inside. They walked past me and entered the basement. A few seconds later, he came out and told them he'll be back.

Our walk was filled with silence. I was thinking to myself, this guy is going through a lot. Just then, a reflection of my past reminded me of my past struggles. Somehow, I noticed his pain was drawing me closer to help him.

I began to fall in love with Nasir, to the point where I was making a decision on apartment rental for him. I didn't like the idea of him living with his cousin. I didn't feel safe being around so many guys. He would oftentimes tell me they would protect me rather than hurt me. Therefore, I became very trustworthy of them, while still keeping my distance. Our conversations were always centered around our families and friends. I didn't have friends, only acquaintances through work and school. I felt like I knew him, so I opened up about my son's father, and our relationship. We got closer each day and started to share our past issues.

I felt so connected and it felt peaceful whenever I was around him. I looked forward to talking to him each and every day and just being to be myself. Honestly, it felt like we were made for each other. I had grown to love him, just as much as I did with Nathaniel and probably more. I had never experienced a real love relationship. Everything was going great and felt like a dream.

Even though Nasir knows I had a child, I hadn't introduced Sergio to him as my boyfriend or his stepdad.

Over the next few weeks, we continued in our relationship and I would have visited him whenever I got a chance. One day while we were watching TV, he leaned over to kiss me. I leaned forward and embraced the kiss, since it had been a while that I was in an intimate relationship. Additionally, I asked him to wait for the real hardcore part, then we both laughed and said ok.

In a few months, I would be starting Audrey Cohen College in Manhattan. Classes was three days a week. I decided to pursue my Bachelor's Degree in Accounting. Once I'm committed to something or someone, I will see it through all the way to the end. With working a job and going to school, I know that our time together will be short. Therefore, I tried my best to share most of my days off with my son first and in the night time to communicate or visit Nasir later on that night.

Several nights all I wanted to do is hit the books and sleep. College was no joke. The professor was harder on me than my mom. There was no excuse for late assignments, but tonight all I wanted was to see Nasir.

So I called him as I got off the train and told him I was stopping by for a little before I pick up Sergio. I must have been there for almost three hours cuddling and watching movies. Just as I was leaving, his oldest daughter called, this time I was able to converse with her for awhile. I could tell by our conversation, she was a smart young lady. She had also hoped to meet me one day. I told her yes for sure on my next visit, I will.

I had so much love for his girls, to the point that anything he needed for them, all he had to do was ask.

Few months into our relationship, I noticed a change in his behavior, he became controlling and possessive. Doing crazy stuff, like taking away my cell phone, always checking on me whether I'm at work or school. And I know for sure when a man starts doing these things, it's one of two things, he's doing something or he's about to do something.

It was getting to the point where I was becoming more and more concerned about where our relationship was going. I asked myself if this was the type of relationship that I would like to be a part of. Things were changing for the worse. The fights and arguments were becoming more frequent.

This guy was obsessed with the likeness of me having any type of relationship with his friends, or anyone, everyone was a suspect in his mind. But whenever I knew he was carousing around any of the girls. It was okay, we were just friends even when I know that he's actually flirting.

To him, it was all about being a man. To me it was being disrespectful and he thinks whatever he does is okay, but as soon as I do anything, it's a big problem. It is getting to the point where I couldn't have a conversation around him, not even with my friends. It was all about him and nothing and no one else.

I was getting tired of the abuse, so I called the cops on him and they arrested him. That was the first time, my mom knew he was hitting on me. I was scared of him, plus I didn't know what a relationship should look like. I knew he loved me and I loved him too, but I was tired of the accusation and all his lies. He's the one cheating on me with some of the girls in KFC especially one particular girl.

Whenever, I mentioned her name he would get upset and ready to argue with me. All I ever did was love and take care of him. I gave him a job, find a new apartment and new furniture even helped to pay his monthly rent. By this time, I know it's time to walk away. I had no business getting involved with him. His handsome, smooth talking was what caught me. We would fight regularly. He would take my phone or threaten me with his words.

I would leave him and he would find me anywhere I go. I was really becoming traumatized by his behaviour. Everytime, I broke it off with him, he would wait for me at the train station. By this time, I was attending Audrey Cohen College of New York in Manhattan.

Knowing that the only stop for me to get off the train was at 233rd Street then walk to 235th Street. Therefore on Friday, Saturday and Monday, he would wait for me right at the train station. As I got off the train, he would call and I wouldn't answer. So by the time I reached downstairs, he'll try to argue with me, take whatever money I have on me, take my cell phone and just leave. Knowing that I have to come to his house to get my money and my cell phone.

When I got to the house, his cousin was there, I told them what happened. They just said to me, "Finechild, that's between you and Nasir, we're not getting involved." Then one of them said to me, "He loves you man, that's why him behave that way with you." I replied, "You don't love somebody and beat them and fight with them every chance you get, while disrespecting me in front of your family and friends. Then behind closed doors, you're all lovey-dovey with them. I'm tired of it and I'm done. I won't have nothing to do with him and I'm calling the cops."

Nasir would deal with me so nasty in front of his friends and when we were alone, he's either scolding or arguing with me about cheating on him. In his mind, everyone wants me. He was a controlling, jealous and paranoid individual. I was tired of all the accusations, so today I decided I was done and I'm never turning back.

Just then he came downstairs laughing, everything was always funny to him. Sometimes he can be so childish, it drove me crazy. I just looked at him. I looked at his friend and said, "You can keep the money and the phone because I'm done. Goodbye."

Several weeks passed and I thought I was in the clear from not seeing or hearing from Nasir. I was starting to get my life back together, not thinking about him. Suddenly, I received a call from one of his closest friend and family member; that he needed my help with something, and it has to do with his daughter. I have always had strong relationship with his daughters, because I'm a mother and I know what it's like being a single parent. I don't know where there Mom was, but I already have motherly love towards those two girls in Jamaica. The cousin's girlfriend let me know that the oldest daughter was sick and needed to go to the hospital. They needed to transmit some money to Jamaica so that she could go get a checkup. He didn't have it at the time, so he was asking me if I could send it for him.

I was really taken aback, that he had the nerve to even call me. My first thought was to tell him to go to hell. But then I realized the children have nothing to do with our relationship. So I told them to give me all the information that I needed to send the cash to Jamaica so that Kamella could go to the hospital.

That night, it was very cold so I was hesitant about walking to 241st Street and White Plains Road to go to the 24-hour Western Union. I did it anyway because of the love I had for the girls. I sent the cash and then I sent the information over to him so that he could tell the girls to pick up the money. I got a response back, *"Thank you I really appreciate this Cordea."*

Over the next couple of months, my focus was my son and college. I also had a part-time job at The Home Depot in Port Chester. Therefore, being a mom and a full- time/ part-time employee was definitely keeping me busy. One day while I was on the train headed to Portchester for my part-time job, my phone rang. I didn't recognize the number, so I let it go to voicemail. A few minutes later, it rang again and then I answered, but there was silence on the next end of the line. I realize the only person, that could be calling me is Nasir, but after all, it had been months since I had any interaction with him.

I held the phone for a few more seconds then I hung up. I contemplated dialing Nasir, but I decided not to. I just went about my usual day. A few minutes later, I exited the train, my phone rang again. This time it was a different number. I paused for a second and then I answered. I said, "Hello?" Nothing. I said, "Hello?" Then I heard a voice say, "Cordea, can I talk to you?" I looked at the phone in disbelief.

I could not believe that he had the nerve to call and say that he would like to talk to me after everything he did and put me through. I listened again for a while. He said, "Cordea, I know you're there. Can I just see you after work? I'll meet you at 235th." I said, "No, I can't talk to you right now. I'll call you when I'm ready to talk to you," and I hung the phone up.

A few hours later, it was Nasir again calling me. I quickly answered and asked my head cashier for a break. Just as I said, "Hello, he said Cordea I really need to talk to you. Can I come by KFC to talk to you now?" I'll let him know that I'm not at KFC and when I'm heading home later, I will give him a call.

Over the next couple of days, we became friends. We started talking on the phone a little bit more. After all, I was still in love with him, but needed to take some time away from him. One thing we did best in this relationship was converse. We were better friends than soulmates. We spoke about private stuff. Things that I went through with my last boyfriend and our thoughts on life, raising children and our future. I loved talking with him, it makes me feel so much closer to him.

During this time, we decided to reconnect with our relationship. I told him about all the things he did to me that I didn't like. He gave his point of view, which I didn't understand or believe. Somehow like I said, I was still in love with them so it was easier to get reconnected to him. This time we agreed that our relationship would be different. It will be better, there would be no physical contact, and or mental and emotional abuse.

I actually believed him so I decided to give him a second chance. To give this a second round, but if it doesn't work out, then I know it's definitely time to leave. Call me crazy like I said I was still in love. We had always talked about living together, after all I was partially paying his rent. Therefore, I started looking for a two-bedroom in New York. I must have looked at over 50 properties. These properties were above my price point, plus the apartments were small or in a bad area.

Since I was almost finished with my Bachelor's degree, I decided to leave New York and move to Connecticut. I had visited several times and besides, you get more apartment for your money. Although we have talked several times about living together, Nasir was a bit hesitant to move out of New York. He had all his friends and some family members that lived in the area. He felt as if I was trying to tie him down so he told me he was not moving to Connecticut.

I loved the culture and vibes of the area. Therefore, my mind was already made up to move out of New York with or without him because I wanted a better life and structure for me and my child. Nasir was not pleased with my decision. I told him the door will be open if and when he decides to join us.

CHAPTER EIGHT

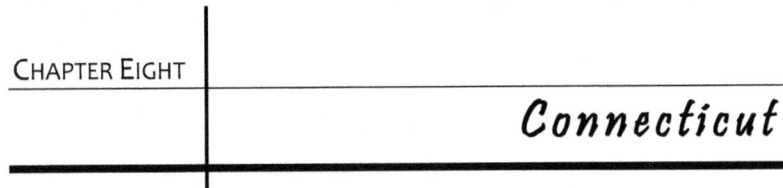

*"And the LORD, he it is that doth go before thee;
he will be with thee, he will not fail thee, neither forsake thee:
fear not, neither be dismayed."*
Deuteronomy 31:8 KJV

It was June 2004 when I transferred from Port Chester, New York to Home Depot in West Hartford. It was closer to my first apartment. My first few days were a bit awkward; I didn't know anyone or my way around the area. Additionally, I had two siblings living in close proximity, but our relationships weren't quite loving. My first day on the job was a breeze. The head cashier introduced me to several of the employees and management. That day was a lot of inside training regardless of transferring to the new store.

While in the break room, a few girls were sitting together talking. By the accent, I could tell that they are Jamaicans. A sense of peace came over me because I could connect with them when the time is right.

Since I was sitting alone, one girl came over and said, *"Hi, welcome to West Hartford."* She asked me where I was from, I told her Kingston, Jamaica, but I had been living in New York for a long time. I decided that I needed a change so I transferred to Connecticut.

Her reply, "*I hope it's worth it,*" and walked away. I was a bit annoyed as to what the hell she meant by that.

At this time, I also had a cousin Julie who lived in the Hartford area. She would come over to visit me and Sergio consistently. We would hang out and just have fun. One day I needed some groceries and she wasn't feeling well. So she told me to drove her car.

She had a black Ford Taurus, and I wondered what would happen if I crashed or got pulled over?

Julie responded that she didn't care if something happened to the car as long as I was okay, that's all that matters. She knows I can drive because while in New York, my brother-in-law had taught me to drive, but I had no driver's license. I said to her, "OK," but before I went around that steering wheel I prayed for a safe ride. I took the car and went to Shaw's Supermarket on Prospect Avenue, I got some grocery, took my time and drove back home in less than 30 minutes safe. Usually, I would walk for about 30 to 45 minutes to the grocery store with Sergio and take a cab back. So today, she made my life easy and I was very appreciative of the gesture.

When I got back to the apartment, Julie was *like see everything is okay, right? You got back here safe.* I tell her I was nervous since I had no driver's license, but God carry me safe.

Since it was the weekend, I was expecting Nasir to visit as he usually does weekly. After he closed KFC, he would take the Greyhound from NYC to CT and then a cab to the apartment. Additionally, one of the girls from Home Depot invited me to an all- white event on Main Street at the West Indian Club. I decided to go and have some fun, until he gets here around 2:30am, but I would need a babysitter for Sergio. My cousin Julie said she will keep him and I must go and hang for a little while, I was still young.

I was excited. It had been awhile since I went clubbing. All of my party crew was still living in New York. They were afraid to leave the city because they thought Connecticut was country. The truth of the matter is, Connecticut makes you view life differently. There is more to life than keeping up with the Joneses.

All I had to do was shower, I stayed fly. My hair and nails were always on point. I needed to pick out an outfit. Tonight was special. I took out a white short dress that said, *"Go get him girl."* I was in a committed relationship with Nasir, but every now and then you gotta bring out the, freak'em dress.

It didn't take long to get ready. Just as I was about to call a cab, Julie said, She would drop me off and pick me back up. Wow! Talk about a life saver. My cousin was always there for me when I needed her.

Just as I exited out the car, to walk to the front entrance to meet with my co-worker. I heard a group of guys talking. One said, *"Look at that fresh meat, she is beautiful. Watch the knock knee."*

I was here to party, not catch a man, so I held my head straight and smiled, as I reached the door. A few girls were standing waiting to go in. One asked me, "What perfume are you wearing?"

"Issey Miyake."

"Ooh...expensive."

"We gotta have expensive taste."

Just as I walked in the door, my phone rang, it was my co-worker, saying, *"Girl, where are you?"* I said, *"I'm here at the door."* She said, *"Wait there."*

I waited for a few seconds, then she walked up to me. Her face was in awe. She said, yes, *"Omg! You look hot bitch."*

I smiled and said, *"Thanks, but I ain't a bitch."* She apologized and said, *"Let's go have some fun."*

She introduced me to her gang, they were a bit scary. Some had cuts in the face. You could tell they had had a rough life. Not my cup of tea, but I decided it was one night. These girls ain't my friends. I was dancing and enjoying myself, then she asked if I wanted a drink. I told her no and I would get my own, when I'm ready. She said ok and that she was just asking.

I think she noticed that I was not your regular club chick. I moved differently with style and class. After all, my nickname is Finechild.

After a little while, I checked my Movado watch. It was a quarter to 1am. I was gonna party till Nasir reached Connecticut, then I would take a cab home. Soon after, I asked one of the girls beside me where the restroom was located. She showed me to the left of the bar and I thought, great it was all in one spot. I don't like to walk around too much in clubs because guys would normally get wrong intentions. I go to clubs to unwind from the cares of life, they go to get woman.

As I entered the restroom, the same girl from earlier came in and asked, *"You Shaniaue friend?"* I asked, *"Why?"*

"She bad news, be careful."

"Thanks."

I exited that bathroom with a bit of fear. I walked over to the bar and got my Alize drink. As I headed back over to where the girls were, this guy grabbed my hand and said, "Browning, mi need you in my life. I love your moves."

I flashed his hand off me and said, "I don't need you, I got a man," and walked away. Just then Shaniaue met me halfway and whispered in my ears, "Girl, what's wrong with you? You know who that is?"

"Nope, I don't and I don't care."

"He's the baddest drug dealer in Hartford. What he wants, he gets?"

"Oh really, but I'm not on the menu."

"You crazy," and walked away.

Ok now, I feel like I need to get out of here. It started to feel like it was a bad idea, so I nudged her and told her I'm leaving. She said wait, she would get me a ride. I told her I will call a cab.

I exited the club to go outside. Just as I reached for my phone, it vibrated. It was Nasir so I answered. He was at the bus stop in downtown Hartford. I told him where I was and to let the cab pick me up. I could tell he was pissed, by his response, *"What the f*** you doing at a club?"* and hung up.

I waited outside. Shaniaue came out with her girls and asked if I was ok. I told her yes. I'm waiting for my boyfriend to pick me up. She said, *"OK, but that guy wanna talk to you."*

"What guy?" The guy I told you about earlier. In a few seconds, he exited the club and came over to where we was and he asked me where I lived, so he can give me a ride.

I told him I was ok. Just as he reached out to hold my hands again, a yellow cab pulled up. I know it was Nasir. Additionally, I said good night to everyone, excused myself, and entered the cab.

I could tell Nasir was furious with me for two reasons, what I was wearing and me going to the club. He sat in silence all the way home. As I exited the cab, he said to me, *"Pay the man."* I looked at him and said, *"OK,"* I paid the driver and walked away. Before I reached the apartment door, he grabbed my hand from behind so hard that I cried out in a loud voice. Then he said, *"Shut up! You think I didn't see your man?"* I was like what man? I don't know the guy. He grabbed the key from me and opened the door.

From the minute we entered the apartment, we were physically fighting and screaming expletives for at least an hour or more. He would hit me so hard, that it hurt like hell, but I would hit him back and even bite him. It made no impact, his hits were deadlier than mine.

After we finished fighting, he wanted to have sex. We fought some more because I wasn't about to have sex with him tonight after he just beat the crap out of me. The next morning I woke up as he was still laying in bed, I slowly drifted out of bed. I got up and walked in the bathroom, checked out my face and it was bruised from him hitting me in my face. I cried for a little and then sobered up. I walked in the kitchen, took out the biggest knife and walked in the room slowly. I attempted to get closer to the bed, but he had turned around. Now he was laying on his back, yet still sleeping, so I stood there for a moment.

Contemplating, if I should I just threaten or stab him, but the thought of my son Sergio caused me to drop the knife on the floor. The room was carpeted so he didn't hear it fall on the floor. I quickly picked it up and carried it back to the kitchen.

From that day, I told myself I was out. Never again would I allow a man to hit me.

Chapter Nine
Pregnant & Alone

*"Trust in the Lord with all thine heart;
and lean not unto thine own understanding. In all thy ways
acknowledge him, and he will direct thy path."*
Proverbs 3: 5-6 KJV

It was two weeks later, before I had any interaction with Nasir. My feelings for him had diminished. I finally realized that he was not the man I needed to be with. I didn't want to continue in an abusive relationship, with a cheater and a liar. Besides, I couldn't continue supporting his financial needs. He never bought me anything in our relationship.

I can't believe I stayed in it for four years with limited love and lots of abuse. I was the idiot who kept giving him a substantial amount of money and or paying for material things. I know it wasn't a self-esteem issue. I had great standards for myself, but commanded very little from him. I was getting tired of my own excuses for his behavior. Enough was enough.

So, I made a decision this weekend when I visited New York, I would talk to him one last time about my feelings. Sometimes, I asked myself, why it was so hard for me to let go? I didn't know what love was. I knew I loved him and the intimacy between us was fire. That was my only answer.

I must have called and texted him over 10 times, still no answer. This was the day he should have returned from his trip to Jamaica and Miami to see his families, on my dime. That night I knew something was wrong and Nasir was ignoring me. It's the weekend, time to party. I couldn't wait to finish my shift. I will be going to New York to get my hair and nails done and to hang out with one of my friend, Yanique. We had planned to attend a pink and white party in the Bronx.

Enroute to New York, he called saying that he wanted to see me. I told him that we could talk. I've been trying to get in contact with him for several days now and I will be in New York, so I'll give him a call. When I got there, before or after the party, he was very upset when I said party. He was like where you going? What kind of party? You are leaving your house all the way in Connecticut to come into New York for a party and he just hang the phone up on me.

By the time I got to New York, it was 5:30pm, I had enough time to change my clothes and meet up with my friend at a beauty salon.

In a few hours, I was ready for the club. Yanique met me at my mom's house and from there we took a cab to the lounge on Gun Hill Road. As we exited the cab, my phone rang and it was Nasir. I didn't answer, I had no time for the drama. Tonight was a night to let go and be free. A few hours had passed since I came into the club. I felt someone tap me on my shoulder. I turned around and it was Nasir. I was shocked to see him there.

I didn't know that he was coming to this party. He said to me, *"It's time to go. I'm taking you home."*

He started to get aggressive with me and I was afraid of him hitting me in public, so I told Yanique, I would see her later and I just walked out of the club in front of him. As I exited the club, I noticed one of my guy friend at the corner. He said to me, *"Finechild, you leaving so soon?"* I told him yes and I would see him tomorrow. By this time, Nasir was in my ears. He asked me, *"Who's that guy?"* I said to him, *"He's just a friend."* He said, *"Okay, we'll see about that."* By this time, there was a cab parked outside, waiting for us. As soon as we got in the car, he punched me in the face. I screamed out and held my face. The cab driver asked if I was okay? He replied, *"She fine, just drive."*

I sat there in complete silence, thinking how can I continue to allow him to abuse me? This is not love. I finally built up the courage to tell him it's over between us. He looked at me and laughed like it was a joke. This guy will never let me go. How many times I've tried to leave him with no real result. He always comes back. A few minutes later, we arrived at the apartment. I exited the cab first and tried to walk the opposite direction to get away from him. He grabbed me so hard. I turned around and hit him in the face. He was shocked that I hit him, so he grabbed me by my hair and pulled me towards him and said, *"Get your ass in the house!"*

A few hours later, it would be Saturday morning, so he told me I was spending the weekend with him. I told him I needed to go in the morning, to pick up Sergio and go home. He laughed. This always annoyed me. Whenever it came to anyone, but himself, nothing was ever important or serious. He was one selfish, controlling man.

A few months had passed and we barely spoke or saw each other. For once in my life, I felt safe and at peace.

As I was on the bus to work, I felt nauseous. I thought that maybe the ride was to long. I had always had trouble with long distance travel, I got nauseous and sometimes, I vomited. So I reached in my bag for a mint and was started to feel better. My phone rang and it was Michelle asking if I was going to work. She would pick me up if I'm ready. I told her that I was already on the bus and almost at work. I told her I wasn't feeling well, but I should be okay by the end of the bus ride. She said okay she'll see me at work and should be able to take me home since we're closing together. By the time I got off the bus, I was still feeling nauseous and now dizzy. I now realized that I was having symptoms of pregnancy. I thought to myself how could I be pregnant? It had been months since I'd been intimate with Nasir. Anyway, I dismissed the thought out of my mind, maybe I'm just not feeling well, maybe it's just because I'm tired. I went on to work, but throughout the day I was still not feeling well and I couldn't wait to go home.

I was only two hours away from ending my shift, when I felt like I needed to vomit so I ran to the bathroom. I spent a few minutes in the bathroom thinking to myself what was this? *Oh my gosh, I can't be.* It had been 10 years since I had a child, I didn't want to go back down this road, but whatever the Lord's will, I'll deal with it.

When I left the bathroom, I went to find Michelle. I told her that I think I'm pregnant. She laughed at me and said, *"Girl, stop playing. You're not ready for that yet, you just getting on with your life."* I asked if she could stop by the pharmacy on the way home, so I could get a pregnancy test? She laughed at me and said, *"Okay girl, whatever, stop."*

I was feeling nervous as I took the pregnancy test. It was one of the most confusing time's of my life, as I waited the required time. The plus sign was getting brighter. I damn near fell on the bathroom floor. I was shocked and confused. I did not want to be pregnant, no not now and definitely not for Nasir. I ran out the bathroom, got dressed and went to the pharmacy which was right there on the corner of Farmington Avenue and Prospect. I purchased three additional tests because I was still in denial from the first. A few minutes later, I was in the bathroom again. My phone rang. It was Michelle calling to ask me about the result. I did not answer the phone because I still didn't believe it myself. I sat on the bathroom floor for about an hour. I know for one, I'm not going to have an abortion. I was a single mother before.

I was really confused. How can I get pregnant while on birth control? I know nothing is 100% but I was on depo-provera . How is this possible?

Today, I decided to call Nasir, I called his cell phone and there was no answer. I called back again, right after still no answer so I just left it alone. I went about my usual day, but I was just thinking about what I'm going to do, first things first. I needed to call the doctor for an appointment, to find out how far I am and stuff like that. She knows, that I am on birth control and I was still seeing my menstrual throughout the last couple of months.

Since it was the weekend, I couldn't call my Gynecologist for the next appointment. Sergio noticed I was still in bed, so he came in to the room. He asked, *"Mom you ok?"* I told him, I wasn't feeling well. He then proceeded to ask what he could do for me? I told him I will be ok, I just need to rest for awhile. Ok mom, I'm here if you need me. I smiled just as he exited the room and said to myself I am raising a polite young man.

A few hours later, my phone rang. I know that it was him calling me back because of the ringtone. Just as I ran to the living room to answer, he hung up. I called back. He did not answer so I sent him a text message to call me I needed to talk to him. I see that the message was read, but he didn't respond.

It was his style not to respond to your text until he needed something. I was still in bed, feeling tired and drained. Then I remembered I did not answer Michelle's call last night. So I called her and told her that I think I'm pregnant based on the four pregnancy tests I took last night. She laughed so hard that I found myself laughing too.

Right in the middle of that, she asked me if I called him?

It was now after 12am early Saturday morning, when I heard a knock on my door, I was a bit afraid to get up out of bed to answer because the only person that came to my house at this time of night was Nasir. And since it's been months since he came to my house, I never thought that he would have just showed up. I continued to lay in bed still wondering who's at my door. I waited in my room for a few more seconds, then I gently got out of bed and checked on Sergio in his room. He was sound asleep. So, I slowly walked to the front door, to listen if it was my door knocking. Just as i reached the door, my phone rang, it was Nasir. I quickly answered, just as I said hello. He said aloud in my ears, *"Open the damn door!"* That's when I realized he was at the door. I hung up the phone and then opened the lock. Just as I opened the door, I said to him, *"How the hell am I supposed to know that you're coming here? Nobody don't come to my house especially this time of night ever, other than you."*

He just looked at me, hissed his teeth and walked right in like he was the man of my damn apartment. I then turned around to lock my door. Just as I walked past him, he then headed straight to the bathroom to take a shower. He had just gotten off work, this was his usual routine when we're together. He would come up every weekend preferably Friday nights straight from KFC and go back down Sunday night.

I went back into the bed waiting for him to finish, so that I can talk to him. After about 20 to 30 minutes later, he walked in the room asking me where's his clothes? I just looked at him and turned my back. Normally, I would have his clothes ready so that when he gets out the bathroom, then I will lotion him down and he'll get dressed or we become intimate. Not tonight.

He hissed his teeth again, while he walked over to the chester draw to take out his clothes.

I continued to lay in bed with my back turned to him, but I could hear every single move. After a few minutes later, he was laying in bed, touching me to turn around to face him. I gently shoved his hands away, as I was not in the mood to have sex with him. I just wanted to talk to him, a phone call would have sufficed.

He waited a few minutes then tried to do the exact same thing as he did before. I then turned around and said to him, *"I'm pregnant."* What happened next was very disappointing of him. He said, *"How? That can't be my baby. I haven't been with you for a long time. So how is that my child? It must be somebody else's."* Right away, he's accusing me of being with somebody else when all this time for the last four and a half years, all I ever tried to do is walk away from the relationship. I never cheated on him and never gave him a reason to think that I would cheat on him and now I'm in this predicament and he's telling me it's not his child. I contemplated my next move. I sat silently for a few minutes, then I told him to get the F out of my apartment. He started laughing like it was funny. Once again, it was so annoying. Never something very seriously, he would laugh about it like it was a joke. So I said it again, *"Get the F out of my apartment. Go get out of here. I will deal with this by myself."*

Suddenly, he realized that I wasn't playing. I was serious. Then he said to me, *"Calm down Cordea, are you really serious? Are you really, really pregnant? How how many months are you?"* I told him I don't know, I just found out yesterday which was Friday and that's why I was calling to tell him that I needed to talk. I never knew that he would have just come up here without talking to me. He then said to me so what are you going to do? I tell him, I don't know I'll wait until Monday to call the doctor to find out what's going on. Nasir started telling me he doesn't want to have a child, he's not ready for a child and he think that I should have an abortion.

I said out loud…, "Abortion are you freaking crazy? I was 15 with my first child and I never thought about an abortion. Why am I going to do that now? I have my own apartment and I have a job, I can do this on my own I don't need you, f*** your help. After all, I take care of you and occasionally your kids in Jamaica. So what kind of father you going to be anyway? You think I wanted to have a child with you? Never in a million years, did that ever crossed my mind. The sex is awesome, but not enough to continue in this abusive relationship and now with a child."

For the rest of the weekend, it was total awkwardness between the two of us. I hated him even more than I did before through the abuse. I hated him because he's trying to take a life out of me. I could not wait for the weekend to be over so he could leave my apartment.

Since it was Sunday and within a few hours, he would be leaving soon. He then told me that he needs money to go back home. I looked at him and said, "Really? You're telling me that I need to have an abortion. It's not your child and you're asking me for money to go back home? Sometimes I think you have no heart. You're such a heartless person and selfish individual." He just looked at me and walked out of the kitchen. A few minutes later, I went into the room. He was packing up his stuff up to go. I said nothing to him. I just let him do his thing. Few moments later, he called to Sergio telling him it will be awhile before he sees him and he must take care of his mom. Then he said to me live your life and walked out the room. I was astonished at his behavior towards me. Never in a million years did I think it would come to this, but if this is what it takes for us to split, then that's what it is. It was a price that I'm willing to pay.

It has been over a week since I last talked to Nasir or seen him. I haven't called him since he left my house, but today is the day that I wish I had someone in my corner to talk to, as I walked out of the doctor's office. Just playing over and over in my head as her words cut through my mind. Saying that I was in my first trimester with a due date on or around August seventh. As I recalled the last time I was intimate with Nasir, it was a few days before his birthday in November. That was our last fight and I decided enough was enough. I know I said it before, but that night as I remember that last hit. It was enough not to go back.

Suddenly, I heard a car horn beep. I jumped and that's when I realized I was about to cross the street on Woodlawn and Asylum. Not paying attention because I was deep in my thoughts. I quickly stepped back on the sidewalk. I took a deep breath and said a small prayer, while waiting for the light to change to cross the street. A few moments later, the bus arrived. I got on the bus pay my fare and walk to the back of the bus. As I sat down, I hung my head down in shame. I was confused and ashamed of my situation. I know that I'm a strong woman, but even a strong woman needs someone to lean on at times.

I sat on that bus for the rest of the journey, all in my thoughts contemplating my next move. I was so deep in my thoughts that I didn't realize that I missed my stop. I was only a few stops away, so I got off the bus and walked back to the original stop to go home. Just as I reached my door, my phone rang it was Ruthy, Nasir's sister. Over the years, we have developed a great relationship. She was my confidant when it came to the intimate details of my relationship with Nasir.

I decided to answer the phone because I needed someone to talk to. Just as I answered the phone, she asked me if I was okay, she hadn't heard from me in awhile? I told her that I am okay, but things are not going so great between me and her brother. She said oh my what's up now it's time for him to grow up. I laughed and then I said to her I'm pregnant, and Nasir telling me it was not his and I need to have an abortion. She was so shocked by my reply, she said you know I'm going to call him right now. I told her no worries, I'll do what I got to do. I don't need Nasir. Then I tell her I'll talk to her later as I was in no mood to talk to anyone. She said, *"Okay, call me if you need me."*

By this time, I felt no need to talk to anyone or get out of bed. I was in a state of depression. So today I decided to call out of work and have some me time after I dropped Sergio off at school. When I got back home, I decided to eat some of the breakfast I made prior, so I grabbed a plate and went straight in my bed. While I lay in bed, I decided to text Nasir. I told him that I was three months pregnant and the baby was due in August. I don't know the gender as of yet, but when I find out, I will tell him. But to my surprise, he texted back I don't give a f***. I must have read that line over 10 times and then I started crying to myself. How could this be? Why is he so wicked towards me? What have I done to deserve this from him? It was then I felt this sharp pain in my heart and I know that my heart was now broken. The love that I had for him, it would never be the same and it was definitely time to walk away. I no longer wanted the boyfriend and girlfriend, baby mother- baby father relationship, any longer. By this time, I hadn't told my mom or my siblings, that I was expecting a second child. I already knew what their responses will be especially my mom because I know that she really doesn't like Nasir for the simple fact that he was very abusive towards me. Weeks turned into months and I was going on with my life as usual. I was keeping up my doctor appointments, but at times it did get depressing, especially seeing other mothers with their loved ones at each appointment. I was jealous. I wanted that relationship. I needed that relationship in my life especially having a second child 10 years later, with no baby father beside me.

I felt like an idiot, to go through this phase one more time, but I've always known that my God would never give me more than I can bare. He had entrusted me with another child's life and I know that He would take care of us. This was my destiny and I was going to embrace it. Embrace it into a better purpose for both me and my children. I was now five months pregnant and expecting a healthy baby boy. This was the day I realized how strong I was and everything is gonna be okay. Suddenly, I felt at peace with myself and the decision I had made.

Chapter Ten

*"Lo, children are an heritage of the Lord:
and the fruit of the womb is his reward."*
Psalm 127: 3 KJV

It was May 2005 when I closed on my two- bedroom condo. This was another happy day for me, but more importantly it was progress in the right direction for my boys. Since I was expecting my second child, I needed to make sure that I was giving my children the best with or without a father in their lives. As soon as all the documents were signed and the ink dried, I was handed a key. This key was so significant in my life, that I burst out in tears. I was reminded of all the struggles, moving from one home to another and how I was homeless for a few hours. But, God! Today, I know I have somewhere to call home and know that my sons will never be homeless. This was surely the day the Lord has made.

They asked if I needed a moment, I said yes. They all excused themselves out of the office, so that I could be alone, as they told me congratulations. A few minutes later, I called my friend to pick me up so that we could go get the moving truck. By this time, I was only a few months away from giving birth to my second child who was due on August 7th. Although being pregnant was no stumbling block for me, I was moving faster than a 16-year- old. All of the apartment was packed up, I was helping to move, lifting and putting boxes in the U-haul van. My friend and her husband told me several times, Cordea, don't lift anything. We will pack up everything for you don't worry about it. I wasn't an infidel, nor would I let them do all the work. I agreed only to lift non-essential items like my clothing and footwears.

That night I could not sleep. I hate to see a messy place. Therefore, I got up and I started unpacking each room separately. The bathroom. The bedroom. The kitchen. The living room. The dining room, within a few hours my condo looked like I was living there for months.

Since it was already morning, I decided to make breakfast for me, Sergio and my friend. Just as I finished making breakfast, the doorbell rang. As I opened the door, it was Michelle she walked in, but was shocked at the same time. As she said, *"Cordea, how did you do this? You didn't get any sleep."* I told her I was so tired, but then I don't like messy place so I decided to unpack. She was so surprised to the point, where she called her husband and mother-in-law to come downstairs to see what I did. They themselves couldn't believe that the apartment was fully straightened up. They asked me how did I do it? without Superman helping me.

We sat, ate breakfast and talked for a while. After eating breakfast, I told them that I was going to take a shower and hit the bed because I was so tired. I've been up for over 24 hours with no sleep and being in my last trimester. It was really difficult to stay up past certain hours. By this time Sergio was waking up, so I asked Michelle if they could keep him for a few hours while I get some rest. Michelle, her husband and her mother-in-law was like the second family that I didn't have. We're a very close-knit family, we shared stories we hung out together so I trusted them keep my son.

Over the next couple of days, everything was going great. Sergio and I was healthy, we were spending much time together. Therefore I can't and won't complain, God has been good to us. Today, I dread going outside; being pregnant in the summer months, is one of the worst things anyone could ever have done to themself. I had to go see my doctor every week since I was close to giving birth. I was feeling a bit tired dizzy and nauseous. Evidently, I got up, got dressed and got Sergio ready. We went across the street and took the bus to downtown Hartford and then took a second bus to Saint Francis Hospital. Just as I was getting off the bus, I heard a guy said, *"Dang Mommy why you do that to yourself? I saw your stomach before I saw you, you got a big belly, I know it's a boy."* I just smiled as I exit the bus and say thank you.

By the time I walked inside to sit down, I was feeling dizzy and nauseous again because outside was so humid. Sergio asked me if I wanted some water? I told him yes to grab a bottle of water from his backpack and give it to me. I almost forgot today was a day that I found out the weight of the baby. All through my pregnancy, I didn't want to know the estimated weight until it was almost time to deliver. Sergio was more excited than I was to know how much his brother was going to weigh. He was trying to measure who was born heavier than who. His birth weighed 8 pounds 2 ounces and 21 inches. I'm the one who was okay with the weight, as long as he's fully developed.

A few weeks later as I was home alone, my doorbell rang. As I looked through the peephole, I saw Michelle with some balloons in her hand. I then opened the door, unbeknownst to me a few of my co-workers were standing in the corner hiding. Apparently, Michelle and my co-workers from Home Depot were planning a baby shower for me. They know that I would be home because I had taken the last month off to rest up and get ready for his delivery.

Even though my condo was filled with my friends and co-workers, somehow I felt lonely. Deep inside, there was someone else missing and it was Nasir. That day we had so much fun talking and playing games. I received lots of gifts, the only thing left for me to buy was a car seat and stroller. I told them how much I appreciate their time and their gifts and I can't wait for them to see Dante.

Within a few hours, my apartment was empty again and in silence. I briefly had a conversation with Michelle telling her how much I appreciate all that she's done for me and the boys. She is the one of the realest truest friends that I ever have and I hope that our relationship will continue to be the same. That night before going to bed, I made sure I bent those knees and prayed. Thanking God for continuing to send His angels to take care of us. Just as I was about to close my eyes to go to sleep, my phone rang. It was my mom asking me if I was coming down to New York this weekend. I told her no I would be taking a break from New York because it was becoming too much for me to walk and to take the train back and forth. She convinced me to come and she would let me get a ride back home. I told her good night and I went to bed.

Today, I decided to take the trip down to New York under one condition. If I would get a ride down there. I was in no shape to take the train as I was close to my due date and didn't want to risk being on the road by myself with Sergio. So I called my cousin Julie asking if she could take me to New York for the weekend, so I can spend some time with my mom and come back home.

When we got to New York, my cousin said she was going to the nail shop and asked if I wanted to come. I told her no I just wanted to go home and lay down. She then proceeded to convince me to go, saying that you don't want to have a baby with your nails not done. I looked down on my nails and then I willingly agreed to a manicure and pedicure. Maybe it would help with this mood I am in.

A few hours later, I was good as new. I was feeling a little bit better. By the time I got to my mom's house, it was almost 7pm and my mommy was not home. It was about 8:30 by the time I was finally ready to go by my stepfather bar on 225th. When we got there, I noticed there were a lot of cars outside. This was nothing new because every weekend, there was always a party or some type of event at the bar. As I walked in, I saw the decorations in blue and it said baby shower. Again, I was being naive as to what was going on. I stood near the entrance door and called my mom over to talk to her.

She asked me what was wrong? I tell her I'm not feeling well. I just wanted to eat something and to go lay down. She then told me to go to the kitchen, to get my food. Once again, this is normal stuff for me, so I was still naive. As I walked towards the back room, I heard, *"Surprise!"* I damn near peed on myself. I did not realize that they were doing a baby shower for me. That's why there's so many people outside. A few seconds later, Nasir walked up to me kiss me on my cheeks. I stood still in shock for a few seconds until he whispers in my ears play along. I had not seen, nor spoken to Nasir in months. The last conversation we had is when he told me that he was not ready for a child and I should have an abortion. That was it for me. I raised a young man without a father and I was willing to do it again.

Once again, that familiar feeling came back and I felt so loved, yet lonely because I know deep within me, I was in this all by myself and Nasir was showing off to his friends. Making it seem like he was Dad of the year. I was happy that I was able to reconnect with my friends and family who I haven't seen in a long time. There was so much food, gifts and decorations, everything was perfect. Just then, my mom announced time to cut the cake. I went over to my mom and ask her who planned this shower, she said it was her and my friends.

Shortly before cutting the cake, mom had me changed into a white formal dress, just a little above my knee. They all wanted me and Nasir to cut cake. The cake was so cute, it was shaped like baby shoes with blue and white colors. I was so disgusted with the phoniness, it started to show on my face. They asked me what's wrong? I told them I was not feeling well, was nauseous and need to go lay down.

He offered to take me to my mom's house, I really wanted to ride with my cousin. Again, I was playing the role acting like everything was okay at this baby shower. Trying to make everyone feel comfortable. Additionally, not to sense the real truth of what's really going on with this pregnancy, Nasir was good for acting I gave him an award. The ride to my mom's house was very silent. I had nothing to say to Nasir. It had been almost three months since I last talked to him, he didn't call and or check on us.

He realized I wasn't saying anything to him, I was not the usual Cordea who would call and argue with him, this time I was silent. He started making small talks, like how I'm doing? How's the baby? My response was we're fine everything is okay. Then he had the nerve to say you see you need to cut the b******* out I'm trying to talk to you and you over there with an attitude.

I just looked at him and said really Nasir, you over there and act like everything is okay between us. Are you truly being the baby father that you should? He looked at me and said, *"Cordea, you don't give me a chance to."* I was shocked that he had the nerve to even say I don't give him a chance to.

He drove the rest of the way in silence, but just as I reached my mom, building he popped his door open, and walked around to the other side to let me out. At times, he can be real nice, other times an asshole. Sometimes I think he was bipolar. I got out of the car and walk towards the building. Then he said to me, come to Brooklyn tomorrow.

A few days later, I was home cooking in the kitchen when I suddenly felt like I peed on myself. I look down and noticed that my water broke. I quickly called Sergio from his room and told him to dial Michelle's number and tell her to get downstairs right now. Suddenly, I was feeling pressure in my stomach and the pain was becoming unbearable. I know it was time to give birth so I dial 911. The ambulance was there within minutes. They asked me what hospital I would like to go to I told them Saint Francis. By this time, Michelle was already downstairs getting Sergio ready, and then to drop him off my sister Chantal. She told me not to worry, everything will be okay, she will be there as soon as possible.

Honestly, I was feeling a bit nervous and ashamed at the same time to know that I'm about to have a second child and the father is not around. While in the ambulance, I dialed Nasir to let him know I was heading to the hospital to give birth. Nasir responded without excitement and then I hung up.

The lady in the ambulance realized that I wasn't feeling comfortable, she told me that everything is going to be okay don't worry about it, I'll be in good hands. By the time I get to the hospital, Michelle was there, making sure that everything was okay with me. She stayed with me for a few hours until it was almost 10pm. Dante still was not born yet, he was giving me a hard time I was dilating, but not dilated enough so that I can start pushing. It was not until after Michelle left and my last check-up with the midwife, she told me get ready for time to push and she wanted me to follow her lead.

A few minutes later, it was time for the grand entrance. After several minutes of pushing, Dante Moore was finally born at 11:07 p.m., weighing 7 pounds, 14 ounces and 21 inches. He was one healthy baby and that's all I ever ask of my Lord. The doctor slapped him on his butt, to make sure he was okay. He screamed. They checked him out and after a few minutes, he was wrapped in a swaddle blanket and lay down on my chest. It was such a peaceful and joyful moment, I didn't remember the pain that I just went through. I can't believe it has been two days that I gave birth to Dante and there was still no sign of Nasir. I called him a few hours after Dante was born to let him know that his first son was here, safe and sound. Once again, he just said okay with no emotion or anything, that was it and hang the phone up. My sisters, mom and my friends all came to the hospital room to visit. At one point, I had over 10 people who came to look for me in the room. It was a happy moment for all of us, they're happy for me and the baby.

However, prior to my discharge, I had to fill out the birth registration form. I was feeling a bit emotional as I thought about all the things that I've been through with Nasir. To know that on one of the most important days of his child's life, he was nowhere to be found. He had definitely shown me which side of the fence he's on. If he really wanted to be in Connecticut, then he would have taken the train. I hold my head up high and filled out all the necessary paperwork with pride.

A few hours later, I was being discharged from the hospital. Michelle came prepared with the car seat, blanket and everything that I needed to go home. I felt secure, loved and truly blessed to have a friend who never leaves my side.

It has been almost a week since Dante was born and there was still no sign of Nasir or even a phone call. I was determined that I was moving forward, I'm never going to give him a call or do anything at all. I'm a strong black woman. Dante had his first visit to the doctor, within a few days to make sure that everything is okay. I do remember this process as I recalled my mom took Sergio for his first appointment. His checkup went fine. All vitals and everything was in order. He even gained a few ounces, I know that breastfeeding was good, but at times painful. Suddenly, the Dr. asked how I'm doing. I told her that I was fine, but sometimes I feel a bit depressed. She asked me what caused those feelings. I told her just the thought of being a single mom and knowing that your boyfriend is nearby, but he's nowhere around.

She advised me that I needed to call my doctor immediately for a checkup. I told her that I'll be fine, it's just the mood that I'm in and will be okay. After a few weeks going back to work was extremely difficult for me. I had no other financial support, but I had to get back to reality. I will need one or two sitters for the boys. Luckily for me, Michelle's mother-in-law was still visiting from St Lucia and she offered to take care of them. Once again, I am blessed by angels. I felt more safe and secure knowing that the boys will be in one place with people that truly love us. After being back at work for a few days, I was getting home sick and missing my boys. And not only that, I had a new manager who changed my schedule every week. I no longer had a set schedule, and this was very strenuous on me. I had no car and several times I had to take a cab from West Hartford to East Hartford on the nights that I closed the store.

Tonight, while standing at the front end, I made a decision that this was the last night, I'll be closing Home Depot. It was time for a career change, I wanted something in the corporate world I had always envisioned myself. Around the desk and or having my own company and it was time to make this goal a reality.

Financially, Home Depot was not covering my household expenses. I was always a saver, so I know that I will be covered for the next few months and or years, but that would deplete my funds. I needed to make some wise decisions.

Oh my where did the time go? Dante was growing so fast, life was going great, it was just me and my two boys, just enjoying life and doing what we do best. I continued to work at Home Depot while I pursued other job opportunities. At times, I still felt a sense of depression and sadness about my life, being a single mom and a young mom with no father figure around for my boys, but I've always known that God would not give me more than I can bare.

The next couple of months, it was extremely hard to embrace the fact that I was truly a single parent again. My heart hurts, I never quite understood the reason for Nasir's behavior. We had a great relationship, apart from the physical and mental abuse side of it. I was always there for him and his daughters. What I did not understand was the nature of his relationship with his firstborn son? I know that he did not want to have a child at this time. At times, I felt like I was forcing him to have a relationship with his son. It seems like I wanted the relationship more than he did. So over the years as Dante gets older, I began to realize that our relationship was fun while it lasted. Some people come into your life for a season and for a reason, you just got to realize when it's time to let them go.

I made a commitment to myself and to my sons, that I would never get into another relationship or introduce them to anyone unless I know that it's for real. I will know when it's for real because this time I will pray for the right man to come into our life. I know that he will be a man of God and I also know that he will not be perfect, no one is , but more importantly he would love me and my children as if they were his own flesh and blood.

I am a Strong Woman, but even a strong woman needs a strong Man by her side.

Chapter Eleven
Stalker in My Building

"Two are better than one; because they have a good reward for their labor. For if they fall, the one will lift up his fellow: but woe to him that is alone when falleth, for he hath not another to help him up. Again, if two lie together, then they have heat: but how can one be warm alone? And if one prevail against him, two shall withstand him; and a threefold cord is not quickly broken."
Ecclesiastes 4:9-12 KJV

It was November 14th 2006, as I exited my apartment to go to the corner store. While walking down the hallway, just as I passed a red door on my right. I heard a noise behind me. I had never seen anyone enter from that door. A young man entered from that door and since It was late, I took my phone out and acted as if I was on it.

I continued walking down the hallway and then I exited out the front of the building. A few minutes later, after getting my phone card to call Jamaica, I decided to walk around the courtyard to get my mail. As I opened up the door, there he was, the same guy from earlier. He had on a yellow polo shirt. Somehow that yellow shirt looked great on his chocolate body.

I opened the door and retrieved my mail. Just as I went up two steps, he asked me a question.

"Do you live in the building?"

"Why?"

"I like you and I wanna get to know u better."

"Really?"

"Can I have your number?"

"I have two boys."

"I love kids."

He gave me his number and just as I walked away, he said talk to you soon. I smiled and said goodnight.

As I walked back to my apartment, I was thinking to myself. What does this guy want? I had two kids and I could clearly see that he's younger than I am.

I went about my business that night, put my kids to bed and it was now time for some me time.

Prison Break was my go to escape of my reality to being a single mom. I like the drama and anticipation, this made it so intense to watch. A few days later, I decided to call Dwayne. I retrieved the number from my contacts. The phone must have rang, but it seemed as if he answered it in five seconds.

"I was waiting for your call."

"Really why?"

"I really like you and I meant what I said the other night."

"hmmm..."

"How old are your boys?"

"10 and 1."

"Big gap, when will I get to meet them?"

"Hold on, we not in a relationship, nor do I introduce my boys to anyone."

"You gonna be my wife. I loved you from that night."

OK, this is creepy and crazy."

"You believe in love at first sight?"

"Nope, never happen to me."

"Please believe it, cause it's true. I love the way you carry yourself."

"Yes, I'm protective of my boys. I might be a single mom, but not a foolish one."

"See, that's the reason why I love you."

How come I never saw you in the building before?"

"I work nights, so mostly during the days, I sleep."

"I can't work no nights, I love my bed too much."

Laughs

"You do what you have to do to survive."

"Well it was nice talking to you. I gotta go now, gotta go cook dinner."

"Wait and you cook too?"

"Yes…"

"OK, can I get dinner for lunch later?"

"You serious?" "Yes, can you call me at 9pm to wake me up and I will get ready and meet you in hallway."

"I guess that's ok."

"Thanks babe."

"What?"

"Thanks babe."

"Bye."

Ok, this must be a movie, this guy is crazy. What was I thinking? All these thoughts possess my little mind. He loves me. He loves kids. He wants dinner. Love at first sight. Wait his guy trying to use me.

So, I called my best friend Michelle, who also lives in the same condominium. I told her everything. She listened and laughed at me. Cordea, you being paranoid. I was like, *"Girllll you hear mi say him loves me. Dude don't even know me."* Just then she said to me. *"You said you want a husband right? You remember your prayers and our conversation? This might be your answer."* I said to her, "Dwayne is nothing like the man I envisioned my husband to be. I like them light skinned. Tight jeans hot boy looking Jamaican. You know the gangsta type." Michelle laughed at me and say now you sound crazy. We both laughed and said later girl.

I cleared my thoughts and went ahead and cooked dinner that night. I had made some curry chicken, white rice and mixed vegetables. I also set my alarm on my phone to 9pm. I called him at 9pm., woke him up once again, as the phone rang he answered. He said he's going to take a shower, get ready and he could meet me in the hallway before 10:15pm also is there a way that he could call me back. I said no, I will call at 10:10pm when I'm leaving apartment.

We met up, I handed him the container, he smiled and said thank you and said he loves me. He walked away. I stood there for awhile feeling a bit numb as to what just happened. It was Thanksgiving Eve when Dwayne called and asked me what was I doing for Thanksgiving? I told him that I'll be going over to my sister for Thanksgiving, and I will not be home until Friday evening.

He sounded a bit sad, I asked what's up? He said he would love to spend Thanksgiving with me and my boys. Also, he wanted to go to New York to see his family, but he was too tired to make that drive.

I felt sorry for him. The holidays were a time that you spent with your family. My plan was already made so there's no way that I could have changed it. Additionally, I haven't even invited him over to see my boys, we met in the hallway daily so I could give him his dinner before he goes to work.

I apologized for not being able to spend the holidays with his family or with me and my boys, but, he already knew the circumstances around my boys. He said ok and good night and hung up. Honestly, I wasn't thinking too much about him. So, I went ahead and continued packing me and my boys bags to go enjoy our Thanksgiving with my family.

A few weeks passed since I met Dwayne. We began our relationship as friends. Therefore, we spoke several times during the course of the day. We spoke about our past, past relationships or families. I mentioned about my two baby fathers, Their lifestyle, how they treat my boys and how I'm a single mom, not working, but I'm very independent and can take care of my own. I guess we are both looking for someone that we could talk to.

He was determined that I was gonna be his wife, so he said if I ask you to marry me. Will you? I paused and said I might think about it, but I honestly, don't want to rush into any commitment so soon.

"He will ask my mom for my hand in marriage."

"You don't even know her?"

"I will one day."

"He loves everything about me, my character, the love for my kids and that I'm a family person. I am independent. I'm strong and he gotta have that sister in his life."

I Laughed. I still wasn't taking this serious at all.

We continued to talk about each other's lifestyle and what we hoped to get out of our relationship. We both have been through so much in the past. Honestly, the conversations were real. I never thought I would have unleashed so much baggage of the past, with someone that I just met. I guess I felt very comfortable talking about past hurts and how I used those hurts to grow into my purpose.

It was Christmas Sunday 2006 and I decided to go to church with Michelle and my two boys. We decided on that church with a purple bus in the East Hartford area named New Testament Baptist Church. We attended service that Sunday and the Sunday church service was different for me, as I've always been to majority of black churches. The church family was very friendly and welcomed us warmly.

The church service ended about quarter to 1. As we drove home, we talked about the church, saying this is not what we expected, but we did like the service and would visit another time. We drove home together and later on, I had dinner with Michelle, her husband and her mother-in-law. I told Michelle that I've been speaking to Dwayne and how he told me that we are going to marry. I was a little bit amazed by his character his love and for me and my boys, it was just like love at first sight.

Michelle said to me stop complaining and embrace it. I must remember our conversation. That I want a man, husband and father. That God answered prayers in ways we can't fathom we both laugh and said let's change the subject. Ma, (Michelle's mother in law), joined the conversation. *"You know Cordea, he might be the one for you."* I said to her, *"Ma he's a Gemini and he's younger than I am."* There's no way that I could be with someone that's younger than me. Besides, I'm still thinking about how I'm going to introduce him to my boys, because I'm not ready to be in a committed relationship. I just wanted to focus on my life with my boys and find a job.

Michelle replied, *"Okay Cordea, keep praying."* I said to her I will. As we finished our meal, I had to change Dante's diaper. He had just woke up from the ride home from church. Afterward, we played Ludi and we also watched a few TV episodes. By the time I realized it was almost 9pm and I was still upstairs at my friend's house. I said good night, got my boys together and went downstairs. Since we already had dinner it was very easy to put them to bed.

Now it was my turn, daily I have some me time where I reflect on my day. Write in my journal and think about my life, what I wanted to accomplish in the future and what I wanted out of life.

A few days had passed and I hadn't spoken to Dwayne. He would call, but I wouldn't answer. I was just trying to reflect on my past and how to move forward. Additionally, deciding on how different it would be from previous relationship.

Now it was Christmas Eve and with all the holiday drama. I forgot to call Dwayne. I was busy shopping and decorating for me, the boys and my brother who was living with us at the time.

My doorbell rang. I said who is it and it was Dwayne. He was standing at my door with gifts. I smiled and said sorry I haven't been returning your call. It's just been crazy busy for me. He said it's okay and asked if he could come in. I told him my boys are up and it was just not the right time, for him to meet the boys and I wasn't ready for it. He said to me that he understood and leaned forward, kiss me on my forehead and handed me the bags and said he'll talk to me later.

I stood at the door amazed and I couldn't believe what just happened. He wasn't upset. I closed the door and put the gifts under the tree and that's when Sergio came around the corner and asked, Mommy who was that? I told him it was a friend, he said okay and what's for dinner?

I smiled because that boy is always hungry. There was a period in my life that I was glad that I had trusted God to see me through. I wasn't working, barely receiving an income. Therefore, I was also receiving Food Stamps from the government to fill the gap until I got employment. At first I was embarrassed, yet grateful to get WIC, Food Stamps and Health Insurance. Whenever I went to the grocery store, it felt like I was being revered by others as a individual that lives on welfare, but wears expensive clothing, and had no ambition. Therefore, I only shopped late at night when the store was empty. It is a cold world when someone falls and no one to help lift them up.

Dinner was ready in about two hours, we got together said grace and eat. We talked, played games and watched television, but before bed, I called Dwayne to check on him. He answered, he wasn't home alone, I felt better, he was in New York with his dad, step mom and brother. As I tried to get off phone, he wanted to talk about our future. We spoke that night until Christmas morning 4am.

It was January 1st when I decided to evolve into a relationship with Dwayne. My focus for 2007 was to get closer to God, find a job and embark on a new journey. So I called Dwayne and asked him if he could come by the condo, so we could sit down and talk. My boys were away with my sister on New Year's Day. I was going over later to have dinner with them.

He said he would in 25 minutes. I said ok and continued to straighten up my apartment. I don't like a messy place. I believe it's a reflection of who you are and how someone views you.

A few minutes later, my bell rang. I opened it and invited Dwayne in as he entered my apartment, he was amazed at how traditional and clean my apartment was with two boys.

I smiled and said welcome as he removed his shoes. Such a gentleman, that's one of my pet peeves… I had a two-bedroom, but my living and dining area was the center of the apartment. I had red and black leather chairs with a chaise, a 60-inch Samsung Television, (the one with the big back and heavy like a deadman), yup that one. My table was square shaped glass with black and red leather chairs with circles on the inside.

I must say, my little space was comfy and looked like it belong in a home magazine. Dwayne loves it and just as I motioned him to sit, so we could talk. He walked towards me, kiss me on my forehead and said you gonna be my wife one day. I know it. Again, I must admit this is getting creepy. He constantly mentions this when we having a serious discussion and part of me was getting annoyed, but loved it at the same time, (weird right)?

I smiled and said that's why we need to talk.

That day we talked about us and my boys, what our commitments and obligations mean to each other. How I'm going to deal with my boys, my family and stuff. We spoke for a very long time, I didn't realize it was almost midday and I needed to go get my boys. He asked me if he could come with me to visit my sister. I called my sister and asked her if I could bring my friend since I needed a ride over, she said yes. I introduced Dwayne to my sister and my two boys as my friend, as I should anyway. They all said, "Hi." The boys continued playing together until dinner was ready to serve.

As we sat, prayed and eat, my older sister is very inquisitive, she asked a lot of questions, to gain knowledge of who he was, where he's from, who his family was and what he does for work. At one point, I was so embarrassed and felt it for him because she kept on going. To my surprise, he was very patient. He didn't seem annoyed by answering the questions. He was just ready to answer everything she asks him with a quickness. It felt a bit awkward like he was being interrogated.

February 2007 was a very special month for me. I was baptized and became a new creature in Christ. Additionally, we decided and committed to each other to be celibate until the day of our wedding. It was very hard at times, being around each other, but as I stated before, I was taking things one day at a time and let God and life draws us closer.

Sometimes, I pull away feeling like we moving too fast, besides my friends and family didn't believe us that we're going to be celibate until we get married. That was a difficult moment. We thought that they would be happy for us, but we know what we wanted and nothing or nobody will make us compromise that. It doesn't matter to us what others think, is what we believe for ourselves.

Truth be told it was the most self-centered, motivated, and agonizing part of a relationship, but we did it.

What people don't realize is that there's so many ways that you could be intimate with someone without actually having sex. By doing so, you get to learn and love the individuals for who they are. Additionally, the conversation will be so intriguing. You get to know each other and enjoying those moments of togetherness. I fell in love with my husband and I thank God for him daily.

It was a big gathering at my home for the Easter celebration. We had a full house which consisted of my siblings, friends and my mom came to visit from New York.

Everyone was at the right place at the right time, to hear this wonderful news and congratulate us on our new journey.

On this day, Dwayne decided to ask my mom for my hand in marriage. My mom was impressed by his principle and his courting ideas of being celibate until we get married. However, no one believed that we could have done this. They were a little skeptical about our relationship since Dwayne was four years younger than I am. Everyone was wondering what he saw in me. To have to want to marry a woman that has two kids and the first child could not have been his child because of the age difference.

Sergio wasn't quite pleased about this concept, as it had been me and him for over 10 years. So this is new for him to have a stepfather or dad in place. After a brief moment, my friend Michelle broke the silence, that we had for a few moments. You can tell everyone was in their thoughts, processing the news. She said, "You know what's crazy is I can see the love that Dwayne has for you just by looking in his eyes and everything will be okay." A few weeks have passed by everything was going great in our relationship. However, Dante's father decided he wanted to see Dante. He occasionally saw him when he sees fit and it's convenient for him.

He will take the drive up to see Dante, (Heading to Boston with friends), on this specific Saturday he decided to see him for a few hours. He asked to come by the apartment to pick up Dante. I told him no problem, I'll bring him downstairs. However, while downstairs he asked to use bathroom. I told him okay because I didn't see anything wrong with it, but unfortunately for me, he was being disrespectful to my now current boyfriend Dwayne. He came into the apartment and walked around the house as if he owned it, then asked where the bathroom was. I showed him the bathroom and he went in. He had no regards to Dwayne being there.

He looked at Dwayne and walked out, I went behind him along with Dwayne, and we went downstairs to put Dante in his car seat. While doing so, Nasir came behind me as I leaned forward to strap Dante in. I turned around and pushed him away, this was an awkward and embarrassing moment for me, but I know Nasir was just being an asshole.

Afterwards, I was heading back to the building where Dwayne was and he said to me, you see that. I don't like it and you need to put a stop to it. I answered. I agreed. That's how Nasir is, especially because he sees you around, so he's trying to make you jealous.

It was close to my birthday and we are both the Gemini zodiac sign. Dwayne didn't celebrate his birthday or Christmas to get a present. His response was as long as he's with me and the boys, he's ok. I told him he's a bootleg Gemini. I loved my gifts and it had to be expensive. I was still into material clothing and stuff. Dwayne brought me several Diesel and Armani pieces of clothing plus jewelry for my birthday. We had a candlelit dinner at home with the boys. That night was fantastic. We all had fun, eating and entertaining each other.

Afterwards, we chatted for awhile on the thought of him moving in and giving up his apartment. We lived in the same building, but he spent most of his awake time with me and the boys. He was becoming a household name.

So that night we talked about the benefits of us living together and continued our celibacy, which will definitely be a test of our relationship. Especially sleeping in the same bed. A few months before our wedding, Dwayne lost his job. I was a bit devastated and sad. I had just started my job at Waste Management and had only been there for a few months. Now the tables are turned, I'm working and he's not. We came together as one and tried to make things work on one income instead of two. As you already know previously, Dwayne moved in with me a few months prior, so our bills were combined.

I was worried while Dwayne was acting like nothing happened, He just said to me, we will be ok and to continue planning the wedding. Nothing was going to stop us from getting married in November. My response was God knows best. So let's just trust Him and I walked away. It was then he entered our bedroom and whispered in my ear. Whatever Cordea wants, she gets. I will move mountains and do two jobs if it makes you happy, I would do anything for you.

I turned around slowly, then kissed him on the forehead. And said, I know you love me, but I don't want you to over kill yourself to make me happy. We in this together. He smiled and said that's why I love you. We decided to seek Godly counsel prior to marriage. We made an appointment with my current Pastor, as I was a member of New Testament Baptist Church. At this moment, Dwayne was not a member yet. However, he occasionally came with me to Sunday School and or service, while discussing our future plans with pastors and how we wanted to be counseled by a man of God. As we hoped to have a Godly home and marriage. He advised us that he would only marry us, if we wasn't living together.

Dwayne will have to move out in order to continue counselling. We both were shocked at the response. However, we both did not agree with his decision, but respected his standards, thanked him for his time and left his office. Going downstairs we spoke briefly, and said to each other, we will not stop at one, we will seek counsel at a different Church of the same authority. Later on that day, we went to Zale's to preview wedding rings. I chose two rings that I loved and hoped that he will purchase the heart shaped one for my bridal ring. After all, I'm the one wearing it. Through counseling, I learned that I will have to compromise and agree to disagree with my soon to be spouse. It opened a lot of my thought process, also it was then that I realized that my past, can and will interfere with my future. I will not allow it to define me. Being a single, independent, strong, Black woman and to be transitioning into a role, where you have to be vulnerable, submissive and informative to another individual. It is not an easy task, but the reward is so much greater. We continued our counseling session, additionally, while hearing negative comments from our own family members towards our relationship, Dwayne was four years younger than I was. Therefore, I was reminded of it frequently. He's too young, can he support you and the boys and the list goes on. My advice was let me make my own mistake and we will find out with or without all the judgements.

But one thing is for sure, one friend had my back, she said forget everyone and just elope. Honestly, I was entertaining the idea, but all the planning and ideas I had for our wedding, no one was going to come against them and take that away from us.

The day is finally here, November 17, 2007, was one of the happiest days of my life, along with giving birth to my boys. I thought on this day, nothing could go wrong, but to my surprise, my veil was ripped and my dress wasn't pressed properly. Therefore, we had to take it back to the cleaners. Just as I was going down Burnside Avenue, my husband to be was coming up Burnside Avenue. We literally passed each other.

I was three hours late for my own ceremony. Dwayne was being patient, but a little worried. The best man advised of the issue that we were having with my gown and that's why I was running late. When I got to the church, all my family and friends were there waiting patiently. We proceeded the ceremony with a prayer, Psalms, and 2nd Corinthians 13, the love chapter of the Bible. We also had a lighting of unity candle. We concluded our ceremony, as the psalmist said, *"This is the day that the Lord has made let us rejoice and be glad in it."* I was surrounded by families, friends, neighbors, and strangers. Additionally, most of all, we was with people who loved us. As you can imagine, lots of pictures were taken, we received so much love and praises from our guests. Our reception guest list was over 100 people, but 98 showed up. Everything was perfect, just as I had envisioned it. Everyone was happy, the children were having a blast with the music. We had a fabulous, fantastic, wonderful, and amazing night in the presence of the Lord.

From our wedding day until now, we stay grounded on our journey of husband and wife.

ROMANS ROAD TO SALVATION

Disclaimer:
Not imposing my religion on anyone, but I do believe that there's a God in Heaven. The creator of all mankind.

"For all have sinned and come short of the glory of God."
-Romans 3:23 KJV

"For the wages of sin is death; but the gift of God is eternal life through Jesus Christ Our Lord."
-Romans 6:23 KJV

"But God commendeth his love toward us, in that while we were yet sinners Christ died for us."
-Romans 5:8 KJV

"That, if thou shalt confess with thy mouth the Lord Jesus, and shall believe in thine heart that God raised him from the dead, thou shall be saved. For with the heart man believeth unto righteousness; and with the mouth confession is made unto salvation."
-Romans 10:9 -10 KJV

God Bless You.

About the Author

A Woman of God, Mother of four, Wife, Prayer Warrior, Author, Entrepreneur, Speaker and Philanthropist. She is currently apart of a Skincare Company. Cordea has shared her story on several platforms such as local community channel in her area and through speaking engagements. She is currently still a member of New Testament Baptist Church.

She is currently pursuing her Bachelors in Science in Accounting. She is also currently pursuing her Real Estate licensing in Connecticut and establishing her non-profit organization in 2020.

CONTACT CORDEA

For Speaking, Workshops and Vending opportunities please feel free to contact me:

Website: www.cordeareid.com

Email: cordeareid@yahoo.com | creidtlc@gmail.com

Facebook: Cordea Reid

Instagram: finechild4

www.ingramcontent.com/pod-product-compliance
Lightning Source LLC
Chambersburg PA
CBHW070551170426
43201CB00012B/1809